Best Wishes,

Linda Maddox

Rosalynn:
Friend and First Lady

Rosalynn:
Friend and First Lady

Edna Langford and
Linda Maddox

Fleming H. Revell Company
Old Tappan, New Jersey

Scripture in this volume is from the King James Version of the Bible.

Library of Congress Cataloging in Publication Data

Langford, Edna.
   Rosalynn, friend and First Lady.

   1. Carter, Rosalynn. 2. Carter, Jimmy, 1924-
3. Presidents—United States—Wives—Biography.
4. Langford, Edna. I. Maddox, Linda, joint author.
II. Title.
E874.C44L36   973.926′092′4 [B]   80-36861
ISBN 0-8007-1132-7

TO

Beverly, Judy and Jack, Jim, and Lucie,
for encouragement and support during the
campaign months and in the creation of this
book

Bob, Andy, Ben, and Elizabeth, for love
and understanding during the writing of the
book

Jason James and Sarah Rosemary, for
whom, most of all, this will record the flavor
of the history of your heritage

Contents

Foreword

Edna Langford is my friend. She also happens to be my son's mother-in-law, my grandchildren's grandmother, and my daughter-in-law's mother, but she is first of all, *my* friend. We have shared much more than just a family relationship. It would not have been the same for me without Edna. We have done things together that neither one of us would have done alone.

Her book brings back so many memories for me, so many reminders of the great times and good friends we have shared. She remembers all the details: the leaky water pumps, the endless index cards, the butterflies, and everything else. I could always count on her to come when I needed her and to figure out something to do when the luggage was stolen or our driver overslept or someone was rude. Her sense of adventure, and her feeling that we were doing the right thing at the right time, never failed.

I'm not sure that anyone can ever tell the whole story of any presidential campaign, but Edna has told the part of the story I know best. We started out together in the very beginning, and she has a special remembrance of our first friends, the people who took us in, who listened to our story and sent us on our way encouraged; people who let us know Americans wanted the kind of leadership, the kind of government, the kind of hope that Jimmy Carter could provide. In a very real way, our story is their story, too.

ROSALYNN CARTER

Acknowledgement

To each of those people we met, from Homestead, Florida, to Madewaska, Maine, and Aliquippa, Pennsylvania, to Ponca City, Oklahoma, whose story we have not told here. We have not forgotten you and our visit with you. We have not forgotten your kindnesses and loyalty, nor will we ever. You will always remain a part of our lives. Your counterpart is here in the teas, the coffees, the luncheons, the innkeepers, the radio stations, the newspaper offices, the television stations, the shopping malls, the filling stations, the factories. . . . ;

To you who continue to work in the 1980 campaign with the same interest, enthusiasm, and support as you did in 1976;

To each of you whose ready conversation, time, and advice made the memories come alive—especially Betty Gail and Gay Gunter, whose enthusiasm from the first 1966 campaign through the final chapter here have kept fires lighted;

To each of you who helped with the practical logistics of writing and copying and mailing and calling: Karen Scantlin in Washington, who added baby-sitting with the Maddox's children to her secretarial duties; to Faye Prather and Carolyn Boswell in Calhoun, who typed and listened and cared; to Ginny Reese, who for twenty years has contributed her many talents and the love of a sister to all my projects; and to my mother, Dorotha, and my husband's mother, Kate, whose daily concern and insistence kept me on track!

Then to Bob and Linda Maddox, my pastor and his wife—both my friends. Bob saw what Rosalynn and I were doing as unique in all of history *while* we were doing it and started its recording even then. Linda, my coauthor, used her vast labors and talents made it real. Such patience, devotion, and love will seldom be repeated anywhere for any cause!

And to all of you who read this book: Realize the desire with which it was written, understand a little more our First Lady, who has a little of each of us in her, and love her and support her as she supports our great country's President.

Edna Langford

1

Now We Can Do Anything!

"WE CANNOT STAND idly by while an entire nation starves to death. We must cut through red tape and bureaucratic tangles to meet the needs immediately." With deep emotion and an almost indignant anger, Rosalynn Carter spoke to the audience. In the midst of the easy splendor of the State Dining Room, surrounded by some of the nation's most distinguished humanitarians, she was the Rosalynn I knew. Her anger stirred me; her commitment inflamed mine. Her grief, evident in the TV newscasts from Thailand, was marked on her face as she made the moving appeal for aid for the Cambodian refugees.

One week prior to this occasion, Rosalynn had called and invited me to attend some scheduled events in Washington. In order to have a car during my stay in the capital, I drove up from Calhoun, Georgia, my hometown. As I made my way up through the Shenandoah Valley and neared Washington, I thought ahead, to that white and green city that has become more important to me since Rosalynn and Jimmy have lived there. Our grandson, Jason, knows that he is in Washington when he spots the Washington Monument. Before he was two years old, he called it the "mona-monament."

Even though I have driven many times through the massive, iron gates at the southwest entrance to the White House, I always feel a sense of history.

But that day in early November, 1979, I had no time for enjoying the sense of history or the fountains or the sculptured lawn or Jason's "mona-monament." The guard looked at my driver's license, opened the gates, then made a sudden motion for me to hurry through. Glancing into the rearview mirror to see what was happening, I noticed a flurry of activity behind me, and in through the still-open gates swept the First Lady's mini-motorcade. She was on her way back from a memorial service for Mamie Eisenhower.

As I stopped at the diplomatic entrance to the mansion, Rosalynn walked quickly to my car and said, "For a minute, I didn't know what Georgia senator's car was driving into the driveway." My husband, Beverly, a Georgia state senator, has a legislator auto tag. "Leave your luggage and go to Jimmy's office with me. The ushers will help you get your things later. I've decided to go to Thailand, to see the refugee problems for myself. Now I want to talk with Jimmy about it."

As we took a shortcut across the grass to the Oval Office, Rosalynn began to tell me of the urgency she felt about the people in Cambodia. A combination of events had converged to persuade her that she needed to make the trip. Watching television reports of the starving refugees pouring across the Cambodian border into Thailand stirred her deeply. She and Jimmy discussed the problem and knew Americans would help, if they understood the crisis. Jimmy had already met with a group of religious leaders, to announce a program of aid to the Cambodians. Also, as Jimmy and Rosalynn talked further, they considered inviting some national leaders to the White House to discuss the Cambodian crisis and focus national attention on it. During a weekend at Camp David, Rosalynn had received a call from a member of the National Security Council who thought it would be very helpful if she went to Cambodia. But Jimmy's reaction was negative; he felt it was too dangerous for her to go there.

The needs of the refugees had been on Rosalynn's mind for several weeks, and the anxiety she felt could not be dismissed. When Billy and Ruth Graham were overnight guests in the White House, they, too, had discussed the situation in Cambodia and ways to aid the refugees. Later

Rosalynn met and talked with people from the International Red Cross and UNICEF, along with many others, to learn what was being done and what needed to be done.

On this Monday morning, November 5, 1979, before Rosalynn left for the memorial service for Mrs. Eisenhower, Jimmy told her the Thais were becoming nervous about the refugees from Cambodia that were pouring into their country. He felt something had to be done to bolster the Thai government and give it moral support. So, following this conversation and reflecting on all the other related events, Rosalynn decided to go to Thailand.

As we walked into the Oval Office, we met a group familiar to us: Hamilton Jordan, Jody Powell, Jerry Rafshoon, and Jack Watson were completing a meeting with the President. Following a brief exchange of greetings, with an edge of excitement in her voice, Rosalynn explained her decision: "I want to make the trip to Thailand, to see the refugee problem for myself."

Jimmy, standing close to Rosalynn, with his arms folded and a serious expression on his face, said, "I don't want you to go to Cambodia. It is too dangerous and too politically complicated. Now, going to Thailand is a possibility, but if you go, it's imperative that when you return, some concrete action be initiated immediately. Something specific must be accomplished." It was evident that Rosalynn's safety and the condition of the starving refugees caused the President deep concern.

Color rising in her cheeks, Rosalynn reminded Jimmy that the trip would tie in with her long-standing emphasis on volunteerism. She had already been in contact with agencies and individuals anxious and willing to lend support to such a project. In fact, many people were eager to accompany her on the trip.

With that, Jimmy asked, "Who is going with you, and when will you leave?"

The situation was critical. With Jimmy's "Go" signal, plans immediately began to fall into place. Rosalynn and I followed Jody Powell to his office, where he began to make notes as he reached for the telephone. Cables and conversations rapidly began to move back and forth between Washington and Bangkok.

Ideas tumbled over one another as we conversed together while walking from Jody's office, out past the Rose Garden, toward the First Lady's

East Wing office. When I came to Washington, I had no idea I'd be
listening to Rosalynn talking about a trip to Thailand. As always, her
excitement was contagious. I knew she was the right person in the right
place!

At 7:00 o'clock Wednesday morning, the motorcade left the South
Portico of the White House for Andrews Air Force Base, after a short
press conference, held by the President and First Lady. Just before
takeoff, I hurried aboard the plane for a last few minutes with Rosalynn
and other friends. With somewhat of an ache in my own heart to go, I
said good-bye and Godspeed. Later, standing behind the press rope,
watching the plane leave the ground, I experienced the excited anticipation this mission of mercy was generating throughout the world. I
breathed a deep prayer for all aboard. This journey must succeed!

The next days, I listened intently for all the news from Thailand.
Watching the televised segments of Rosalynn's walk through the camps
at Sa Kaew, seeing her lift those babies in her arms, was almost more
than I could bear. I felt with her, when she cuddled them; I felt with her,
when she gave food to a small, emaciated child. When Rosalynn knelt
to touch the sick, giving them words of encouragement, she spoke for me
and for all people in America. As she stood at the microphone, I knew
what she said flowed from her own pain and distress. Tears ran down
my cheeks as I watched. For a long time, I could not talk about that
scene or remember it without deep emotion.

Rosalynn, my friend, was also my representative to an unbelievable
and crushing human wasteland. Her words and emotions became a
bridge between the uprooted people of Southeast Asia and those of us
in America with the compassion and resources to respond.

When she returned four days later, I went in the helicopter to Andrews
Air Force Base with the President, to meet her at 10:30 P.M. In spite of
jet lag, emotional fatigue, and the grueling, no-frills, fifty-eight-hour
fact-finding trip, Rosalynn was anxious to tell Jimmy all she had seen and
done and to lay out her specific suggestions and plans for helping the
refugees. In fact, after a few brief words of greeting, the rest of us were
quickly forgotten as she and the President sat together in the front of the
helicopter lost in conversation. The eagerness with which they greeted
each other, the absorbed way Jimmy listened, the careful manner in

which Rosalynn detailed her trip, were right on target for them. *This is their relationship,* their way of doing things.

As public leaders, a major source of their strength in difficult times is their strong faith in, and love for, each other. They receive courage and confidence from each other to undertake and complete difficult tasks. Their show of mutual affection and respect is not a "made for the public" scenario. It's the real Rosalynn and Jimmy relationship, which has been tested over the years.

A few days later, I sat in the State Dining Room with Rosalynn and those who accompanied her to Thailand, as they reported to representatives from major relief agencies. One speaker after another applauded the First Lady's ability to translate the needs of the thousands huddled in hastily constructed Thai refugee camps into precise terms that would lead to viable solutions. These diplomatic, medical, and logistical experts openly expressed appreciation for her willingness to spend hours walking through the camps, making quick assessments of the problems, asking pertinent questions, being the catalyst for formulating relief plans, and most of all, entering deeply into the suffering of individuals.

The speakers at the White House meeting described the Rosalynn I know: imaginative problem solver; political strategist; compassionate human being; First Lady; yet, through it all; Rosalynn Smith Carter, from Plains, Georgia.

*   *   *   *

These events stemming from the Cambodian refugee problem are typical of the many experiences Rosalynn and I have shared during the past fourteen years.

My mind flashes back to that vivid scene in the Omni International Hotel, election night, 1976. At 4:00 A.M., Mississippi's vote made Jimmy Carter the next President of the United States. We were all exhausted, emotionally drained, but I'll never forget that moment. Rosalynn, in a gray-blue sweater and corduroy slacks, put her arms around me and said, "Now we can do anything!"

2

Jimmy Who?

ON A BEAUTIFUL spring day several years ago, as I was getting ready to go outside and weed the flower beds around our terrace, I answered a knock at the back door. "Are you by yourself?" It was Rosalynn. Before I could nod, she burst into tears.

"What's the matter? What's happened? Come on in!" This was a sight I had rarely seen! The pressures at the governor's mansion had built up. Rosalynn had slipped away without her state-trooper escorts and driven to Calhoun. She had her cry—just as we all must, on occasion. We talked out her problem while we spent the rest of the afternoon weeding the flower beds together.

Rosalynn and I share many things: tears, laughter, clothes, travel, friends, religion, politics, and children. With my husband, Beverly, and me, Rosalynn and Jimmy share Jason and Sarah, *our* grandchildren— who are the children of our elder daughter, Judy, and their eldest son, Jack.

One of my favorite memories is accompanying Rosalynn to Brazil on the "Partners of the Americas" exchange trip in 1973. When Jimmy could not lead Georgia's delegation, Rosalynn asked me to go with her.

We stayed in the home of Camellio and Janet Steiner in Recife, where we formed strong friendships and gained a good feeling for life in Brazil. We did our best to overcome the language barrier, so we could converse with government officials, visit, and of course, do some shopping.

During an overnight side trip to Salvador, adventure turned to anxiety when the fire alarm sounded in our hotel room. All the pajama-clad guests hurried out into the night air, amid the clang and clatter of arriving fire trucks. Luckily, the "inferno" was discovered to be nothing more than a trash-can fire, probably started with a carelessly tossed cigarette. When the "All clear" sounded, we looked at each other, hesitated a moment, then burst into laughter.

Some of our fun moments together have been spent doing really feminine things, like trying on clothes. Rosalynn, Judy, and I wear approximately the same size. In addition, Rosalynn and I share an almost never-miss sense of what clothes the other would buy or wear. Such a feeling makes shopping for each other possible. I selected the pale-yellow dress Rosalynn wore for Jack and Judy's wedding.

When Rosalynn lived in the governor's mansion in Atlanta, Jack Moses sent boxes of clothes from his shop in Americus, for her to try on. One day, while Rosalynn, Judy, and I were having a good time trying on some styles and deciding what to wear to coming events, Chip, our audience of one, half jokingly suggested, "Why don't you swap the dresses around among you? They fit all of you, and you often go to different places with different people." So we did that—especially with the long dresses. Eventually, it did not matter whose dress belonged to whom. We knew the dresses were available to each of us.

Of course, clothes have some sentimental value, too. Caron wore Judy's wedding dress when she and Chip married. The dress and accessories are now safely preserved for our younger daughter, Lucie, and Amy, the Carters' only daughter, and Sarah and her generation.

When Rosalynn first moved to the White House, someone asked her, "Whose dress is that?" For a moment she had to stop and think: "Judy's, Edna's, or mine?" Then she laughed, because, of course, the question referred to the designer of the dress, not its owner.

Not long ago, as I came through the receiving line at a state dinner in Washington for Irish Prime Minister and Mrs. Lynch, the President, bragging just a bit, introduced me as the "other" grandmother of his grandchildren. The relationship between Rosalynn and me is difficult to describe. Lately, we have called ourselves co-grandmothers! As far back as I can remember, people who saw us together asked me, "And *who* are *you* ?" The question comes in all shapes and sizes—from young and old, male and female, in whispers and in loud exchanges. In fact, "And who are you?" has become a family joke, along with "Jimmy who?"

*   *   *   *

I first became acquainted with Rosalynn and Jimmy in 1966. It seems like yesterday. It started with a phone call. Bill Gunter, a friend, called Beverly, my husband, to say, "Bev, I want you to come to Atlanta Sunday afternoon for a meeting. Some of us want Jimmy Carter to run for governor, and we want you to help."

Beverly's response was, naturally, "Jimmy who?"

Although we did not know Jimmy Carter, we did know Bill Gunter. Beverly respected his opinion. Bill and Beverly were law-school classmates at the University of Georgia, which for Georgia fans is instant credibility! Bill is a well-known fellow lawyer and a former member of the Georgia legislature.

Georgia Governor Carl Sanders had appointed Bill Gunter and Senator Jimmy Carter to a committee to revise the rules of Georgia's Democratic Party. Mutual friendship and respect developed as they performed their committee responsibilities. When former Governor Ernest Vandiver dropped out of the 1966 governor's race, Bill immediately thought of Jimmy as a replacement and began talking with him and his brother, Billy, about this possibility. The then new and splendid Riviera Hotel on Peachtree Street in Atlanta was the scene for those earliest meetings among the three men. Bill told us that one evening he and the Carter brothers were at the Riviera Hotel, laboring over the idea of a Carter candidacy, when finally they reached a resolute decision: "Let's do it!" Bill Gunter first called David Gambrell, a lawyer and scion of one of Georgia's leading families, to say, "David, we have a *group* here tonight that thinks Jimmy ought to run for governor."

"Well, that's fine," David answered, in his easy drawl. These men agreed to set up a larger meeting for the following Sunday afternoon.

Because of Bill Gunter's recommendation, Beverly, after attending church in Calhoun, drove to Atlanta to meet this Jimmy Carter. Late in the evening, Beverly returned to Calhoun. He said, "Edna, I'm going to support Jimmy Carter for governor. Not only do I respect the men that were present at the meeting, I was genuinely impressed with Jimmy Carter."

With only three months left to campaign, a political crisis had been created when Ernest Vandiver, the leading Democratic candidate for governor, dropped out of the race, leaving Lester Maddox challenging Ellis Arnall, a former governor from the 1940s, and nine other candidates. The mood of the country was rebellious. It was the antiestablishment era; integration was a key issue.

The Republicans did not have a primary. Former United States Congressman Howard "Bo" Callaway was appointed the Republican gubernatorial candidate. Carter's strategists knew that, since there would be no Republican primary, many GOP voters would cross over and vote for a weak Democratic nominee, hoping to elect a man Callaway could defeat.

In all this mix, Lester Maddox, the colorful and controversial Atlanta chicken restaurateur, appeared to be the front-runner. The men who met with Bill Gunter that Sunday afternoon wanted strong, positive leadership for Georgia and believed Jimmy Carter could win and could provide this strong leadership.

The next three months were crucial for the Carter campaign. During this time, Beverly and I joined a group of Carter for Governor supporters and worked ceaselessly. We canvassed, telephoned, and visited. It was during this time that Beverly and I began to know Rosalynn and Jimmy Carter.

Rosalynn and I first met at the Dinkler Hotel—a dignified, aging hotel in the heart of downtown Atlanta. This landmark hotel has been torn down in recent years, but in its days of splendor, it was the scene of many important political strategy sessions. Many are the stories that could be told of life-changing decisions made within its walls.

On this particular day, as I scanned the Carter group meeting at the hotel, I saw Rosalynn, and I thought, *She just has to be that tall, slender, very blue-eyed blond in the pink dress.* I soon found out that lady was *not* Rosalynn Carter. In fact, I don't know who the blond was, nor do I remember the first time I spoke to Rosalynn. But I do know that as I came to know her, I liked her. She was quiet, young looking, friendly, and had a calm, confident air. She seemed comfortable with me and certainly made me feel comfortable. Slowly, I came to see her quiet confidence as one of her greatest strengths. Some describe her as shy. I think we were all shy then, but not for long, because we gained confidence from each other as our friendships grew into lasting personal relationships.

In 1966, Jimmy's earliest supporters came from diverse backgrounds. The eagerness with which we attacked the governor's race transcended our differences and any self-consciousness or inadequacies we might have felt. None of us were experienced politicians, but we learned fast and began to capture a team spirit quickly.

Rosalynn and I have talked often about those 1966 campaign days and their importance to our families. Since the days of that first primary-election campaign, it was made clear to each person in the Carter family that he was needed in the campaign. The children were young, yet they participated in the activities and decisions. Jimmy saw to that. Often he included his entire family in conversations with advisers and others. Rosalynn and Jimmy deliberately planned this all-inclusiveness. No one was forced to campaign, but it was something each could do for and with the family! Rosalynn mentioned one time, "It was so important, as we came back together, to say, 'This is what *we* have done; this is what *we* have accomplished.' "

To this day, family gatherings at the White House, Plains, Sea Island, or Camp David always have a measure of "Remember when . . . " from the days of campaigning. Judy, my daughter, who campaigned in all the Carter endeavors, feels that the kind of political exchange the Carter family has grows out of mutual experiences. Everyone seems to have a story that is similar, and to listen to the others is like having a camera turned on yourself. Believe me, both of our families identify with that feeling!

The backbone of the campaign was the Carter volunteer organization. The state was organized with chairmen in each of our 10 congressional districts and each of the 159 counties. Competition among the districts was keen. We vied for top honors in money raising and volunteer enlistments. A family atmosphere prevailed. There were no smoke-filled back rooms; no alcoholic beverages—by mutual, unspoken agreement. The whole campaign reflected the Carter life-style.

During the ensuing weeks, those campaign activities began to pull together the whole Carter team and, in particular, the members of the Carter and Langford families. No one worked harder than Rosalynn or Jimmy. I can remember Rosalynn sitting on the sofa, stockinged feet tucked under her, with telephone in hand, making those difficult yet very important calls. Or again, I recall her running up and down the back-stairs at the hotel because the elevator was much too slow!

Work? Yes, but also fun—oftentimes lots of it. One day Charlie Kirbo, the lawyer, brought his huge Saint Bernard into the campaign headquar-ters with a Carter campaign hat on his head. The place exploded. There was also a growing camaraderie. Judy, after meeting Jack at one of those early sessions, commented, "I would not mind going on Sunday after-noon, if it were not for that smart aleck Jack Carter." Before the cam-paign ended, however, the two had become good friends, which is putting it mildly.

The people, young and old alike, who worked that hot Georgia sum-mer, felt the deepest conviction that Georgia needed Jimmy Carter. As I think of those who surrounded Jimmy during those hazy months, I think of selfless people who gathered support from every town and city in the state because they wanted the best and believed that Carter could bring about that *best!*

Jimmy Carter had a fine record in his young political career. His influence on the school board in Plains was well-known and admired. He and Charlie Kirbo waged a fierce court battle to have the senatorial election of the Georgia Fourteenth state district of 1962 thrown out because of voting frauds. Jimmy's tenacity revealed his backbone and willingness to see the right thing done, whether it involved himself or someone else. Also, his record in the state Senate was impressive, espe-cially in the field of education. At his own expense, Jimmy had re-searched and then drew up the highly innovative Governor's Honors Program, to encourage Georgia's brightest high-school students to de-velop more of their potential.

Jimmy's personal bearing; his contagious wit; his easy charm; his steellike intelligence; and *most of all,* his unbelievable capacity for hard work, spurred his supporters and workers to push ahead—to talk to one more person before going home, to be up a few minutes earlier, and to give one more dollar to the effort.

Several who joined him in that first campaign have become well-known Americans. One is Charlie Kirbo, the brilliant, slow-talking, fast-thinking lawyer who loves to drive around in his pickup truck. Another is Hamilton Jordan, a young man who worked in the campaign as youth coordinator. My first phone call ever from a political campaign was from Hamilton Jordan. "Just checking on how things are going in the Seventh District!" he said. From that time on, I felt compelled to check on the Seventh District and many other districts!

Those hectic ninety summer days came to a climax on election night, September 23, 1966. The Carters and some friends ate dinner at the Capitol City Club in Atlanta. The evening meal went well. Everyone had a good time, in spite of the knots in their stomachs and the occasional interruptions as one or the other would tune in one of the portable television sets or radios to get the latest results. After dinner, all of them walked to the Dinkler Hotel to join other supporters who had gathered to watch the returns.

As they entered the hotel, Rosalynn looked most attractive in her summer-white shirtwaist dress with its pleated skirt. The enthusiastic but edgy crowd looked no different from other election-night throngs, but there was a difference: This was the *Carter* crowd, made up of entire families who had become a team—a corps of people who had worked tirelessly for three months, personally committed to Jimmy Carter, hoping against hope that he would make it into the runoff.

Jack Carter, at nineteen the oldest son, manned the blackboard, keeping running tallies of the incoming election results. But the hoped for joy was not to be. Frustration mounted and distress became more and more evident as the votes came in. By early morning, the jubilation and hope of the night before had faded, as Jimmy's vote total fell behind those of Maddox and Arnall. The final tally showed Jimmy missing the runoff by about 20,000 votes: close, indeed, considering the total vote count of nearly 79,000 and the short time the Carter campaign had been on the road. But it was still a defeat—a bitter one.

When Jimmy conceded, everyone cried—Rosalynn, Jimmy, Bill Gunter, Hamilton Jordan, John Giradeau, and many of the other tired, faithful supporters who stayed throughout the night. The gall of losing seemed to magnify the depth of the ties that had developed among members of the campaign team. This mutual sharing in the bitterness of defeat was especially evident in Jimmy and Rosalynn's relationship. While losing had always been a possibility, no one seemed prepared for the extreme disappointment and grief. Families had sacrificed, worked, and hoped; now, hopes dashed, they wept.

For days following the election, a funeral-like pall hung over us. Jack Carter, vocally bitter, spat out the anger so many others felt: "How could *they* choose Lester Maddox, less qualified in every way, over my dad?"

The day after the election, Judy, a high-school senior, and her friend and neighbor Jim Purcell, stayed out of school to go to Atlanta with me. School held little interest for them that Wednesday morning. When we arrived at the campaign headquarters, dismantling of the offices had begun. Judy met Jack, and they consoled each other. Jim and I began to help the staff pack, preserving records for another time, comforting ourselves with the thought that this was groundwork for a 1970 race.

Turning a corner into the one private office in the area, I came upon Jimmy Carter, sitting dejectedly on a low stool. Leaning back, grasping one knee with both hands, he looked up at me. As I reached up to remove another chart from the wall, with still lingering disbelief, I said, "Are you sure we've lost? I mean, they can change their minds, you know, and we can put this all back up!"

The now familiar grin flashed. "No, it's real! But save all this stuff. Send everything to Plains." I can still feel the lump in my throat. We were not prepared for the pain of the cleanup operation. Every poster pulled down caused us great agony. We were dismantling a part of our lives, but as we closed the Carter offices around the state, we knew it was only a temporary setback. There would be a 1970 campaign, and we *would* win!

In early September, soon after Jimmy's primary defeat, a dinner was held in Atlanta to pay off the $76,000 campaign debt. Such a "clear the record" event was unheard of in Georgia politics, but Bill Gunter and others who had encouraged the candidacy knew the need to pay it off. They felt it was unfair to saddle the Carters with the load. Besides, they were looking ahead, to 1970.

In Plains, Jimmy and Rosalynn were having their own time of assessment. When told of the proposed dinner, skepticism was added to their thoughts. No one wants to help an unsuccessful candidate pay off campaign debts! Rosalynn felt sure no one except their closest friends would show up at the Dinkler for the dinner, but even so, she made a new green velveteen dress to wear.

To everyone's amazement, the dinner was an overwhelming success. All available space was sold out. Many who came seemed to say, "We wish we had worked harder."

In 1979, Bill Gunter and his friend *President* Jimmy Carter were seated together at the Democratic fund-raising party at the Washington Hilton, which was attended by 1200 people. At one point in the evening, Bill leaned across the table and whispered to Jimmy, "I was thinking of the Dinkler Hotel. . . . "

"I was thinking of the Riviera," whispered the President.

3

On the Winning Side

OUT OF THE 1966 primary defeat came a most significant spiritual experience for the Carters. Soon after the election, Jimmy was invited to speak to the Baptist laymen's organization at the church in Preston, Georgia, a very small community. As Jimmy wrote this speech, it dawned on him: "For my own campaign, I left the home I loved, my warehouses, even my bird dogs. I probably shook two hundred thousand hands for *myself.*"

Right then, according to Rosalynn, Jimmy calculated how many hands he had shaken as he sought to introduce people to Jesus. In the past fourteen years, there were perhaps ten people or so each time the Plains Baptist Church sponsored its annual revival meetings. To Jimmy, this was a shattering comparison. The critical self evaluation propelled him to accept an invitation from the Georgia Baptist Brotherhood to take part in a large evangelistic crusade in New England. In effect, it led Jimmy Carter to a renewed commitment of his life to Jesus Christ.

How did Rosalynn respond to Jimmy's spiritual awakening? She said, "I understand completely how he felt. I was genuinely moved by what Jimmy experienced and was in complete agreement with him, knowing the depth of his new relationship to God."

*   *   *   *

Jimmy Carter began to campaign for the 1970 Georgia governor's race soon after he lost the 1966 election. During this time, the relationship between Jack and Judy continued to develop. On a regular basis (every weekend of her senior year in high school), Jack came to Calhoun to visit. As a result, Rosalynn and I had more frequent contact, especially on the phone.

As Jimmy spoke throughout the state, he impressed another young lady, whom he would eventually get to know better. Annette Davis, a senior at the high school in Arlington, Georgia, served as a hostess when Jimmy came to address the Future Homemakers of America. "Jimmy made a great impression," Annette recalls. "The theme of the banquet was Spanish fiesta. Jimmy spoke in Spanish, not just for the introduction, but for a full two minutes. Everyone was pleased and amused! By the time he finished, they loved him. So did I." But not as much as she would love one of the Carter family's sons, Jeff.

Between 1966 and 1970, Jimmy fulfilled a tremendous number of speaking engagements. While on these speaking tours, instead of staying in a motel in our area, he came to Calhoun and spent the night with Beverly and me. As we visited, we talked often about politics and our families. He told us he definitely intended to run for the governor's office in 1970 and was prepared to work as hard as was necessary to win the race.

Few people realized how many speeches Jimmy was making. Of course, this meant that he was away from home often. This was not easy for the Carters. Jimmy and Rosalynn missed being together. On one occasion, as Jimmy headed back toward Macon after a speaking engagement, Rosalynn decided to meet him. She and young Amy rode the bus to Macon, a pleasant two-hour ride from Plains. Some supporters who knew of the bus ride raised their eyebrows about the propriety of a candidate-for-governor's wife traveling this way. But raised eyebrows have never bothered Rosalynn too much!

A decade ago, more women began to take on real responsibilities in political campaigns. As the election of 1970 neared, women in Georgia began to ask what they could do to help Jimmy Carter. Women in the

Seventh Congressional District, where I live, were especially interested, so I felt Rosalynn could give the campaign special impetus by meeting with them.

We scheduled the meeting in the Red Carpet Room of the Calhoun First National Bank. This room was available to all community groups. But on this occasion, Bert Lance, president of the bank, made it clear that he and the bank would not be involved in politics. People throughout the state were still undecided about a candidate. Former governor Carl Sanders, Jimmy's opponent, had many friends in our area, so it seemed judicious for Bert to stay neutral.

When I asked LaBelle Lance to bring a flower arrangement, she consented, but as she came into the meeting, she said pointedly, "Remember, I'll do the same for Betty Sanders, if she comes here." It's well-known history now, but several months later, the Lances became solid and stalwart supporters of Jimmy Carter's candidacy.

Rosalynn gamely accepted my invitation to speak in Calhoun. When she reached the backdoor of my house that evening, she had a few last-second thoughts about the whole thing. She came in saying, "Really, do I have to make a speech?" In 1966, Rosalynn's campaigning had consisted mainly of shaking hands and giving out brochures. Jimmy once teased her about being rather slow moving, until she had a handful of brochures; then she buzzed through a crowd with lightning speed.

By arranging the tables and chairs in the Red Carpet Community Room in two half circles, with two card tables in front of them, Rosalynn was able to remain seated close to the group as she talked. Dot Padgett and Jackie Lassiter, coordinators for the 1970 Carter campaign, joined Rosalynn and me at the tables.

Speaking was a new adventure for Rosalynn. Her approach that evening was much the same as it is now: simple, warm, and direct, from one concerned citizen to another. Out of the speech emerged her now familiar themes: "Jimmy understands people and knows how to meet their needs; he works very hard and is an honorable and capable leader; he can restore people's confidence in government; people conscientiously involved in government make the difference."

From that speech also emerged her person-to-person style. Today, as she addresses large audiences, she has the ability to bring each individual into the speech, almost as if she is talking one-to-one.

Our second Carter for Governor campaign effort was successful. On election night, September 9, 1970, many joined us at the Quality Inn in Atlanta, to celebrate the Carter victory—our victory. As soon as the results were certain, Rosalynn and I were to meet Jimmy at WAGA-TV, for an election-night special. Without a second thought, we gathered the children and headed to the car. Jody Powell drove us to the studio. As we unloaded, Charlie Kirbo, waiting for us at the door, said, "You didn't all come in one car, did you?" We looked around, and there were Jack, Chip, Jeff, Judy, Jim, Lucie, Jody, Rosalynn, and I. Quickly, Rosalynn replied, "Who would you have left?" Everybody laughed!

Jimmy Carter was inaugurated governor of Georgia January 13, 1971. Grass-roots supporters were so numerous four inaugural balls, at four locations, were held simultaneously. People came from everywhere. Annette Carter remembers this night as her first date with Jeff Carter, her first big political celebration, and the first time she met her future mother-in-law, Rosalynn. Little did she know this was but the first of many gala political events!

Soon after the inauguration, Judy was graduated from the University of Georgia and embarked on a World Campus Afloat Trip around the world. That same spring, Jack returned to Atlanta after three years in the navy. At the governor's mansion one night, he casually asked me about Judy. When I explained that she was on a trip in Africa, Jack asked how he could write to her.

When Judy came home in May, I met her at the Atlanta airport. She was tired, and had a mountain of luggage to collect, but the first thing she did was call the governor's mansion. Jack's letter had made its mark. Jack wasn't there; he was floating on a raft down the Chattahoochee River. Never one to let anything stand in her way, Judy drove back to Atlanta the next day. The two young people began to spend so much time together that it was obvious big plans were in the air.

Our suspicions were confirmed the first weekend in August. For forty-two years, Mr. Henry Gallman, a colorful, spry, bright political enthusiast, had hosted a barbecue at his Murray County country home to celebrate both his birthday and wedding anniversary. In August of 1971, Mr. Gallman was ninety years old. The guest of honor for that year was Beverly, my husband, an unannounced candidate for the Georgia Senate.

Special guests were Bert Lance, master of ceremonies, and Governor and Mrs. Carter.

After a great meal and music by local bluegrass musicians, Mr. Henry gave Bert the high sign to start the formal part of the program. Jack and Judy watched Bert walk to the microphone on the porch of the comfortable home. As he began his opening remarks, Judy whispered to Jimmy, while Jack came over to Rosalynn and me, and then to Beverly, saying, "Judy and I are going to get married." In the midst of this mini-turmoil, Bert, in mock irritation—with genuine concern—tried to shush the commotion behind him.

But the noise quickly elevated, with Rosalynn saying, "I am glad— that's wonderful!"

I was saying, "Do you mean today?" and Beverly, who always cries at weddings, was speechless, too moved to reply.

Jimmy asked Judy, "May I tell anyone?" and with her reply, he walked to the microphone, nudged Bert aside, and said, "I have a special announcement to make. We have just been told that Jack and Judy are engaged!" Everyone was surprised and burst into delighted applause.

Later I asked Judy, "Why did you choose today and this occasion to tell us?"

She answered, "It seemed a sort of typical family event and the only time we had all of you together!" *The Calhoun Times* later carried a picture of Beverly, Jimmy, and Judy, with the caption, "Country Brass." It was a most unusual, impromptu, engagement announcement!

Wedding plans moved from that day in August until November twentieth. Parties for Judy and Jack began in early September. The first was a luncheon scheduled in Calhoun. Judy and Rosalynn were working in Plains, helping at the warehouse during the height of the peanut-harvest, and planned to fly to Calhoun in the governor's aircraft. I expected a call when they landed at the Calhoun airport. As the time for the party drew near, I was getting anxious, but had to run some errands. When I returned home, Rosalynn's car was in the driveway. Rosalynn and Judy had driven the five hours from Plains to Calhoun. Rosalynn said, with a twinkle, "The governor caught us trying to misuse state equipment. The airplane is for official use only, and apparently a bridal luncheon is not official enough." We had a great laugh. Rosalynn wasn't upset; a governor's wife for only a few months, Rosalynn had had no occasion to learn the ramifications of the state policy. This veto of the use of the plane was completely in character with the honest and fair way Jimmy was determined to run his administration. Everyone was thankful that a mistake had not been made through ignorance.

Jimmy and Rosalynn held an elegant rehearsal dinner at the governor's mansion two days before the wedding. As usual on such an occasion, many toasts were offered for the well-being of the bride and groom, with much good humor and warm comments from various family members. Jimmy's comment on his and Rosalynn's love for Judy closed with, "And this is the first time Beverly Langford was ever outtraded." His surprise ending brought much laughter; Beverly's beagle-hound trading is famous.

Jack and Judy planned a simple ceremony, with only family members participating, so a long rehearsal was unnecessary. At one end of the ballroom, we set up chairs to simulate the arrangement of our First Baptist Church in Calhoun, where the ceremony would take place at noon on Saturday. Imagining ourselves at the church, we walked through the ceremony under Judy's direction.

Saturday morning found me racing to Grace Moore's, to have her hem my simply cut chiffon dress. By twelve o'clock, everything seemed to be in place.

Judy chose, for her nosegay and the flowers in the sanctuary, soft, muted, fall-flower tones in both silk and fresh flowers. The lovely old stone church had seen much of our family's history. Beverly, now a deacon, had always attended church there. Our children grew up in this church. Gathered together here for the wedding of our first child was a small group of relatives and closest friends.

Jack's brothers, Chip and Jeff, lit the altar candles; Jim, Judy's brother, lit candles to be used in the ceremony. Lucie came down the aisle with four-year-old Amy, who carried a miniature of Judy's nosegay. This they placed in a gold-based glass dome, to be preserved for Judy.

Rosalynn, in a dress of lace-trimmed yellow crepe, entered the sanctuary down the right aisle, with Jimmy, while Beverly and I entered from the left aisle at the same time and took our places at the front.

Then Judy, dressed in a simple, traditional candlelight gown, with flowers from her bouquet repeated in her hair, came in with Jack.

Throughout the ceremony, Jimmy and Rosalynn, Beverly and I stood with our eldest children. Dr. Charlie Shedd, well-known Presbyterian minister and writer, presided over the reading of the vows. Both Jack and Judy wrote what they would say that day: beautiful words, full of young wisdom and love. All of us were moved. To complete the vows, Jimmy and Beverly each lit a candle and handed them to Jack and Judy. This symbolic act by the fathers said, "As you have been given to us, we give you to each other." Then, in one simple movement, Jack and Judy combined their flames to light another candle, symbolizing the beginning of their life together.

After the service, many other friends gathered for the wedding reception.

Several weeks later, Judy realized she couldn't find the pieces of paper on which she and Jack had written their vows. Somehow, in the shuffle, they had been misplaced. She was so anxious to recover them, but they were not to be found. Surprise! For Christmas, Rosalynn presented Jack and Judy with a beautiful scrapbook of the wedding events, containing newspaper clippings, announcements, invitations, and pictures she had assembled. In the back of the book, in an envelope, carefully preserved, were the vows!

I had found the papers at the church after the wedding and slipped them to Rosalynn. The secret had been ours. The scrapbook, covered in Oriental silk, was given to Rosalynn by a navy friend who had spent the night of the wedding rehearsal at the mansion. Rosalynn has continued the scrapbook tradition since she has been in the White House. Every year, she presents each of her boys and their families and Amy with a scrapbook of the year's events—gifts that will last forever.

Jack and Judy looked for a place to live in Atlanta while Jack worked on his degree at Georgia Tech. Rents were high and navy benefits low. Rosalynn and Jimmy had remodeled an old barn, one of the original buildings on the grand estate where the new governor's mansion was built, to provide barracks for the Georgia highway patrol security officers stationed at the mansion. Using wood from the inaugural platform, the first floor was converted into a one-room guest apartment. Rosalynn suggested that Jack and Judy live in the apartment. Aside to me, she said, "That won't be like living with your mother-in-law, will it?"

The newlyweds were so happy in The Barn, and the Carters were delighted to have them so close. We had all foraged through family attics and basements, collecting things to be used in their first home.

While Jack completed his work at Georgia Tech, Judy used those months from November until September to work on her master's degree in early childhood education. When not in class, Judy spent hours in the mansion, helping Rosalynn. Four-year-old Amy delighted in coming out to the barn to help Judy. She and Amy became fast friends. Jack aided the cause by painting a small wooden box for Amy to stand on, so she could help Judy in her kitchen.

From the day Jimmy and Rosalynn moved into the two-year-old mansion, Rosalynn loved the stately home and enjoyed sharing it with family and friends. She felt deeply that the residence belonged to all Georgians, so she kept the doors wide open to groups and events of every description.

The governor's mansion provided an ideal place for Rosalynn to promote her special social and political concerns. In those pleasant surroundings, she saw more than a few of her priority projects underway or better implemented. Very few government officials, community planners, or philanthropists could resist her combination of genuine concern, anger at intolerable human conditions, charm, and grace. Bureaucratic red tape, barriers of paper and prejudice, frequently gave way after a session in the mansion with Georgia's persistent First Lady.

Many evenings at the mansion were spent with family and friends enjoying dinner and good conversation. The future First Lady of America had found her niche in the political arena of Georgia. She fit well the demanding role of the governor's wife. But I'm sure there were few at that time who had any inkling of what the future held for Rosalynn, Jimmy, and those of us in this circle of family and friends.

4

Picking Up the Pieces

THE DEFEAT IN 1966 also initiated a time of painful self-evaluation for Rosalynn Carter. How did Rosalynn handle that defeat? She went home to Plains, cleaned the house, worked in the yard, which had been neglected for the summer months, washed clothes, and cooked. As she did these tasks, she thought, *What more could we have done? What went wrong? What can we do next time to win?*

People react to defeat differently. Rosalynn, a highly practical person, reviewed thoroughly the various facets of the campaign, evaluated the what-might-have-beens, picked up the pieces, and, with Jimmy, determined to move ahead. It was a case of "In God's own good time." In other words, she determined to overcome the obstacles ahead by doing. There was no dark night of the soul for her. She had no time for that. She had too many responsibilities. There would be another day, if not for the governor's mansion, then surely for other ways to live a full, productive life. She had three boys, a husband, a business, and a multitude of demands that clamored for her attention.

*   *   *   *

It is hard to say where Rosalynn gets her staying power, especially when pressures are all around, but she has it. She is no stranger to grief and crisis. The death of her father when she was only thirteen years old forced her to face some painful realities and taught her lessons in coping with life's problems. Rosalynn's father was confined to bed only a short time before he died. She and her brothers and sister became aware of his illness in July, and he died in October. Only in the last months of his life did doctors diagnose his illness as leukemia, in those days, always a fatal disease. Her father's ill health put pressure on the family in various ways.

During those last months of her father's illness, Rosalynn remembers once having to tell her teacher, "My father was sick all night, and I don't have some of my homework."

With four children, Mrs. Smith, Rosalynn's mother, had never worked outside her home; in fact, she had never even paid a bill. Mr. Edgar Smith had taken care of all the business affairs. As a result, after her husband's death, Rosalynn's thirty-four-year-old mother began to rely heavily on her parents. It was a real blow when, one year later, Rosalynn walked into the hall at home to find her mother sitting by the telephone, crying. She remembers rushing to her mother and saying, "Mother, what's the matter?"

"Mama has died of a heart attack!"

Rosalynn felt the deep loneliness and pain her mother experienced in those days. But with it, she also remembers her mother's faith and how her mother would quietly gather the children together to read the Bible and pray. Fortunately for Rosalynn and her family, they had deep roots in the life and culture of the people from Sumter County, Georgia. That larger community family, that sense of history, the friends who came and went, provided great strength in times of crisis. In a small town like Plains, when death strikes, the aftermath becomes a family and community affair.

I'm sure that through experiencing some of these painful lessons early in life, Rosalynn has learned how to walk with others through their own disappointment and pain.

*   *   *   *

One of the most difficult times for the Carter family, particularly for the boys, involved Rosalynn's and Jimmy's feelings about desegregation.

Through the years, she and Jimmy had taught the children that everyone is equal under God and ought to be equal in society. Prejudice has no place in the life of the Christian and must not be a barrier between people and certainly cannot be condoned by the church. The boys accepted this position, agreed with it, and lived by it.

The difficulties arose when Plains Baptist Church, where they were members, refused to open its doors to all people who wished to worship there. After the now famous vote, some of the townspeople harassed the Carters, an experience that was particularly painful for the boys. Rosalynn, as only mothers can understand, suffered that pain with her boys.

Family is important to Rosalynn, so another difficult event for her to face was the 1978 separation of Chip and Caron. Caron was a member of the family for several years, had campaigned long and hard with the Carter team, and lived in the White House for two years. The separation was very painful to all concerned. Chip agonized over being away from his son, James. The whole thing was like a death in the family. For a long time, Rosalynn hoped against hope the marriage could be saved. But, as in other times when her children had problems, she did not interfere, giving them room to work them out in the best possible way. The day Caron and little James left the White House, no one wanted to be around. Annette and Jeff went out of town. Other family members scattered. A waiter who had grown quite close to James became so emotional Rosalynn sympathetically suggested that he go home. It was a time of suffering for all.

Because one is famous or in the limelight is no guarantee of immunity from trouble, in spite of what many onlookers think.

While living in the governor's mansion in 1973, the Carters faced another critical situation. This one afforded Rosalynn an opportunity to do something, to share in the problem. Judy suffered a very complicated miscarriage. After a few days in the hospital, she went home, apparently recovering with no problems. Within a week, Jack called to say he had rushed Judy back to the hospital with terribly serious complications. Very frightened, Rosalynn and I hurried to Athens, where Jack and Judy lived. As people sometimes unwittingly do, Judy had waited much too long before calling the doctor. It was a touch-and-go situation. Jack stayed with Judy day and night.

To make matters worse, Jack and Judy were in the process of moving to a two-bedroom house they had rented. The house was in a run-down state of repair, and needed things done—such as some holes in the closet walls patched and a lot of painting throughout the interior. So Rosalynn and I started the repairs. We found a used refrigerator and stove and generally tried to get the house in shape while we prayed for Judy's fast recovery. Staying in Athens, we worked like beavers for three days.

Rosalynn was forced to return to Atlanta, to keep a commitment to host a meeting of religious leaders at the mansion. Although Judy was still quite sick, Rosalynn had to be there for that meeting. The leader of the group later told me she had never seen such emotion etched on anyone's face as when Rosalynn asked the ladies to pray for Judy. Jimmy's secretary, calling to check on Judy, said, "When Rosalynn told the governor how sick Judy was, he sat there with tears in his eyes. They are so worried."

Rosalynn demonstrates this same kind of compassion in all concerns. This was apparent when Bert Lance resigned his cabinet post and returned home to Georgia, when Andrew Young was forced to leave his United Nations post, and when other friends in the administration left for one reason or another. Rosalynn missed them and said so. She's not one to gloss over weaknesses or pander to friends at the expense of justice, but neither does she jump to condemn at the first criticism. I've seen her, over and over again, unafraid to face difficulties when she considered it important to be faithful to friends in their hour of despair.

Rosalynn Carter has learned through personal tragedy. I think this is why she has such a strong desire to improve the lot of the handicapped, and why, when she hears of people with crushing problems, her answer is, "Let's find a solution." No one will know the frustration she experiences when she has to say, all too often, "There is nothing I can do right now!"

*   *   *   *

The most common problems for mothers, of course, are those related to the development of their children: times of illness, concern over schoolwork, anxiety over individual and family priorities, and other such concerns.

Rosalynn has tried always to deal with her children on an individual basis, encouraging and yet being honest. Once, when Jack was fourteen, he was worried about his appearance. Thinking he was skinny, short, freckle faced, and ugly, he asked Rosalynn, "Why am I so ugly?" Most of us would say, "Oh, but you're *not*," or, "You're beautiful to me." But her reply was, "You won't always be."

Jack says the answer satisfied him.

On another occasion in his late teens, during a particularly intensive yet typical time of questioning, one day Jack came into his mother's room and said, "Jesus Christ isn't so much. He was a man, like everybody else." "She didn't say a word," Jack recalls. "She began to cry and then turned and went to tell my dad."

Because Amy is the youngest child and has lived much of her life in the limelight, Rosalynn and Jimmy have been particularly sensitive to her needs. Initially, moving to the White House was not a pleasant interruption for Amy. She had already made several moves and was not pleased about any of them, although she had been able to adjust well to her new environment each time. Amy's first move was to Atlanta, when she was three. As they started to leave their home in Plains, she clung to her grandmother, Miss Allie, and cried for her cousin Mandy. Leaving the families and the normal routine was not easy for this three-year-old. But after making friends in Atlanta and enjoying those years, moving back to Plains was even harder. However, once again back with family and friends, she found a comfortable niche.

Two years later, Rosalynn woke Amy up at 3:00 in the morning to say, "Amy, we won. Daddy's going to be president."

It is no wonder that Amy began to weep and said, "I did not want him to win. I don't want to leave Plains!" All the way from the hotel in Atlanta to their home in Plains, Amy was most unhappy.

By the night of the inaugural ball, Amy, though accustomed to the situation, was still not pleased. One picture taken that night showed her sitting behind Rosalynn and Jimmy as they waved to the crowds, her head in her hands, looking very forlorn. However, Rosalynn understood her feelings and gently began to plan a way to help solve the problem. First, she invited cousin Mandy to come spend some time with Amy. Then other cousins and friends from Plains helped her get over those first new days. Fortunately, after the difficult early days, making new school friends and enjoying the excitement of her special new home helped young Amy adjust.

Rosalynn's emphasis is on helping Amy feel right at home. She does not impose a rigid life-style on her. Large parties are not new to Amy, so she is not awed by any of the events. Instead, she is encouraged to attend what she chooses and enjoy herself. From the early days of the Georgia governorship, Rosalynn allowed her to take a book to read, or work to do, while attending a formal occasion. Those situations were too long and tiring for her to quietly sit and listen.

In the afternoons, when Amy comes in from school, she sometimes goes to teas and speaks to guests in her jeans and shirts. The guests seem to understand that she is coming home from a day at school. They understand that she would be very uncomfortable if she had to change clothes for every event. Rosalynn tries to help Amy be herself, to have as normal a life as possible.

5

"Go and Make Friends"

"GO TO FLORIDA and make friends." Those simple words from Jimmy in the spring of 1975 symbolized the starting gun of a race. During the closing months of the Carter governorship, Rosalynn and I talked many times, planning our first presidential campaign trip.

Incredible as it now sounds, those words "Go . . . and make friends" launched us on one of the most uncommon campaigns in the history of American politics. Not that we felt our activities were unique; it was simply a job that had to be done, and we did it.

During those months from March, 1975, until Election Day in November, 1976, Rosalynn and I traveled more than 100,000 miles. We went to the bigger cities, such as Miami, as well as smaller places like Madawaska, Maine. We visited places neither of us had heard of before, let alone visited.

And we did what Jimmy told us to do: We made friends. We met people face-to-face, at small teas and large club meetings. We saw them at courthouses and cow barns. We addressed people on small-town radio and by large-city television.

No matter where we were, we were constantly aware that out there

in another new place were more new people—new friends and supporters. We were constantly aware that we had to move quickly and often,
to reach even a fraction of them. First we met a few, then dozens—
eventually, we met hundreds, then thousands.

Today, as First Lady, Rosalynn still maintains contact with many of
those we met on our whistle-stop trail, though she has said on more than
one occasion that it's terribly frustrating to see those same people only
as they come through a receiving line. Even then, she tries to take time
to say more than the usual, "Hello." As much as her schedule allows,
Rosalynn chats with a warmth that lets them know she really would like
to have a longer visit.

Occasionally she can arrange for more time, as she did for Janine
Patenaude. Richard Patenaude, an active Carter campaigner from 1976,
and his mother both live in New Hampshire. While visiting Washington,
Richard called and asked, "Would it be possible for my mother to have
her picture taken with Mrs. Carter?"

Knowing Rosalynn, I'm sure she remembered the many times Mrs.
Patenaude had housed members of the Carter family or staff members
during the busy days of the campaign. Rosalynn not only invited Mrs.
Patenaude to come, but insisted she stay for lunch. While not able to
extend such invitations every day, the First Lady does not forget her
friends. And she has many friends. Rosalynn made more difference in
the 1976 presidential race than any presidential candidate's wife has ever
made in any national campaign. I believe this came about because of
Rosalynn's uncanny sense of timing. She had the ability to choose the
right time and place for the beginning of Jimmy's critical Florida campaign. She believed the country needed the leadership he could offer, so
she became totally involved.

As I think back to those on-the-campaign-trail days, I smile as I recall
how each trip began. I'd answer the phone. Rosalynn's soft voice would
say, "Can you go with me?" That's how each invitation began, but the
focus was always different: campaigning for Jimmy; to Brazil for the
"Partners for America" program; to Mexico for the presidential inauguration; to Costa Rica. The list grows. And I always try to work things
out so I can go.

Rosalynn no longer travels the way she did in the early campaign days.
As the president's wife, she whisks about in jets accompanied by mem-

bers of the press, security people, and staff that must always be concerned with protocol.

I often laugh at my famous friend. She can drive around Plains and knows the back roads to other south Georgia towns, but that's about all. Since 1977, she rarely drives her own car. While being chauffeured, she usually is involved in conversation or study.

The President does no better. One afternoon, visitors from Georgia mentioned a restaurant in Georgetown and asked directions. He laughed and said, "I have jogged in Georgetown, but I have no idea how to get there. Ask the Secret Service agents. They know the way." One of the things Rosalynn and Jimmy have had to give up is the simple privacy of driving their own cars.

Rosalynn and I have always been comfortable traveling together. We both share likes and dislikes that help make this so: We both like salads, black coffee, and gooey chocolate treats. Neither of us smokes. We share times of total silence, as well as periods of animated or quiet conversation. Sometimes we polish our nails on the way, and always there are a few notes to be written. Traveling today is much the same as in 1975— the transportation is just a little different!

We still think alike: We both work by tackling the immediate tasks at hand. Our political involvement and our family relationship are common bonds.

Over the years I have grown to appreciate Rosalynn's developing self-confidence. Not only her inherent sense of timing and propriety, but also her calm leadership, spills over to those with her. In the early days of campaigning, Rosalynn did everything she could to prepare herself. She has continued that practice. She studies every available document or pertinent report. This thorough preparation, combined with her common sense, gives her what some people would identify as an intuitive feeling for coping with any situation.

She also has the ability to put anyone at ease. Those who traveled with her to Thailand often spoke of the First Lady's self-assurance as she met the royal Thai family and other government officials. She walked through the refugee camps and talked to the experts in relief work with usually keen insight.

One fellow traveler on the Thailand visit said, "There was no doubt who was in charge of the delegation. In every way, Mrs. Carter was both spokesperson for and leader of the mercy mission."

Despite her ability, traveling on behalf of her husband has not been an easy road for Rosalynn. For example, in the early days of his administration, the president sent her on a goodwill tour to Central and South America. This caused some raised eyebrows. Others openly criticized both Jimmy and Rosalynn. Political pundits either cautioned against or flatly decried the decision. However, the president felt the trip needed to be made, and he couldn't go, so he decided to send his First Lady.

Jimmy Carter knew that Rosalynn understood the problems in South America. She also knew what he wanted accomplished. When he asked her to go, she never hesitated. To Rosalynn, it was another "Go and make friends" mission. The end result was a warm, appreciative response from our friends to the south. She keeps in touch with the people she met there, in much the same way that we remain in contact with the friends we visited in this country while campaigning.

Today the woman from Plains, Georgia, has traveled around the world. She's known and admired everywhere. Yet she never set out to be a parade person.

*   *   *   *

When Jimmy spoke those words, "Go to Florida and make friends," we knew it grew out of strategy meetings held with key advisers in January, 1975. At that time it did not take any political wizard to grasp the significance of Florida. George Wallace had carried the Sunshine State in 1972. Although later crippled by an assassination attempt, he still wielded power in the South. Carter and his cluster of confidants knew he simply had to beat Wallace in his own territory if his campaign were to succeed. As a key neighboring state, Florida was the crucial place to begin.

No one who knew the Carters was surprised that Rosalynn campaigned in Florida. Throughout those hectic days, Jimmy remarked to friends that he would win the primary in Florida because he had a secret weapon. He meant Rosalynn. She gently but emphatically conquered the hearts and won the votes of thousands of people there and, ultimately, across America.

Let me tell you, the road was far from smooth. Rosalynn met and overcame continual political opposition from a variety of sources. A typically difficult situation was the fund-raising banquet on March 24, 1975, in Atlanta. The fledgling Carter campaign was always short of money, in those days. The campaign coffers hinged on public support, and the importance of that banquet's success loomed large to the Carter team.

As both Jimmy and Rosalynn knew, rallying support from Georgia was extremely important. Jimmy had been traveling in Iowa, California, and Florida. People had responded well, but this was not enough. He needed his home state solidly behind him. If the banquet succeeded, they reasoned, additional contributions would start filling the campaign chest. It was obvious that the banquet would be the crucial event launching the national campaign for the presidency.

Rosalynn and I, along with everyone in the campaign office, worked for that dinner. The tickets were to be one hundred dollars a plate. When I first heard this, I thought, *We can never do it. Who wants to pay a hundred dollars a plate?* While not voicing my doubts, I mumbled something about not being cut out for this kind of thing. I never did like to sell anything. When I was a little girl, I couldn't even sell Girl Scout cookies!

Rosalynn laughed, "I'm not good at it, either. But we have to do it, anyway."

Rosalynn worked in the Atlanta area and south Georgia. We lived in north Georgia, so that was my area. My husband was reluctant to ask friends to contribute to the campaign, because they had given so generously to Bert Lance's unsuccessful race for governor in 1974. At that same time, Beverly ran for election for his second term in the Georgia Senate and won. We could not have done it without the financial contributions of our friends. Also, in 1970, Calhoun residents, Gordon County citizens, and many people of north Georgia had supported Jimmy Carter for governor.

"So here we are again, asking the same people to contribute," Beverly said in February of 1975. We hated to take advantage of our friendships. Yet, we believed in Jimmy Carter. We also believed that if our state didn't show its support for him, the nation would never recognize him as a viable candidate. Also, we admitted, if the campaign had no money, there would be little use in making friends in Florida.

We had to face facts. "Let's do it," Beverly said, and we both knew it was the right decision.

One of the first contacts I made was a textile manufacturer in Calhoun and a longtime friend. Over the years, I have valued his astuteness. He was a keen political barometer; if he supported a project or a candidate, I knew it was a winner. His reaction would make a great deal of difference to me, because I respected his judgment highly. With some nervousness, I called and explained my purpose.

My friend listened and then said quietly, "My wife and I will be there."

I was elated. I knew my instincts were right. This support sustained me while I battled indifference from others.

I talked to the people in our community. It became obvious that many in our area wanted Jimmy to have a chance to be president, but even as they agreed to attend and paid their money, a question lurked in their minds. A few even asked it aloud: "Does he really think he can win?"

Pessimistic types reminded me that Jimmy was a Southerner: a regional candidate. They said we didn't have a chance. I would not let them destroy my enthusiasm. I was committed all the way. Sometimes I answered, "How do you know a Southerner can't win a national election? And we won't know unless we try."

Somehow I sold tickets. The money came in, slowly at first, but more rapidly as we moved toward March 24. After working especially hard one weekend, I returned to Atlanta on Monday. Although tired, the glow on my face showed. I could hardly wait to tell the others. Rushing into the campaign headquarters, I almost shouted, "I've sold forty-two tickets this weekend! Forty-two hundred dollars!"

In the meantime, Rosalynn—who shared my dislike for selling tickets —was also working hard. One well-meaning aide handed her a gigantic computer printout of the Democrats in Georgia. "You can start calling these."

Rosalynn took the sheaf of names and numbers, thumbed through them, shook her head, then said, "Give me a phone book and a WATS line. I'm going to sell tickets my way."

She stayed on the telephone for hours, calling people in Atlanta and across the state. She told them how well Jimmy was being received in Iowa and other parts of the country. Then, gently but honestly, she would say, "Jimmy needs your support. Please buy tickets and come and support us in this first big event of the campaign."

She got results. Often we were amazed. Many supporters bought ten tickets—an entire table of seats. Listening to her speak, I thought she seemed so self-assured. Once I teased her, "You could sell anything, Rosalynn."

You know what her reply was? "I believe in Jimmy. That's why I can ask people to buy these tickets."

When Rosalynn was in Plains, she drove eight miles into Americus every afternoon to the office of Peek Industries. After they closed at 5:00, she used their WATS line. Sometimes she stayed there until 10:00 or 10:30 P.M., telephoning.

The banquet was held on March 24. Nine hundred guests attended the dinner. We raised money; we had national media coverage; we were on our way!

Jimmy spoke to the enthusiastic supporters, sharing his hopes for our country. After he spoke, people used the words *powerful* and *impressive*. Then it was Rosalynn's turn. I knew how hard it was for her to stand up in front of that prestigious gathering. She was nervous. Later she told me her mouth was dry and she felt her stomach muscles tighten up. But she looked composed and self-assured, and as she spoke of her confidence in her husband, she ended by saying, "And I want you to help Jimmy."

That dinner in 1975 contrasts with the fund-raising kickoff for Jimmy's bid for re-election in 1980. There were 1,800 people present at the Hilton Hotel in Washington, D.C., that night. They paid $500 a plate. This time, Rosalynn did not have to sell tickets, but she did have to speak.

Jimmy couldn't attend the dinner. He was involved heavily in dealing with the Iranian hostage crisis. He had determined not to campaign publicly until a solution was worked out. When she stood before that group, Rosalynn was at her best. Her voice was strong, her words decisive. The next day a leading newspaper in Washington headlined the event. It read: ROSALYNN CARTER—SHOWSTOPPER.

As I think of all the newsmedia covering the 1980 fund-raising event, I remember that only one of the newspapers covering the 1975 banquet even commented on Rosalynn's speech in the next day's paper.

That is understandable; in 1975, no one thought of the importance

Rosalynn would bring to the role of First Lady. She had been a hard-working First Lady of Georgia, but few noticed. Along with her husband, she had been developing leadership qualities during his political life, but few were aware of this. She improved her speaking technique as she appeared more frequently in public. She also learned that even though the press did not realize the value of what she was doing, people listened. They respected her. They began to see, apparently before the media experts did, that the Carters were a political team, as well as husband and wife.

When Rosalynn and I talked about completing plans for our 1975 trip to Florida, the staff looked at us quizzically. "What trip? What plans?" they asked.

They had not only been unable to keep up with everyone's plans, but, outside of Jody Powell and Hamilton Jordan, I don't think anyone had any appreciable understanding of Rosalynn's potential clout. They all focused on Jimmy. It simply had not occurred to them that she was just as much a key figure.

Jimmy had said to us, "Go to Florida and make friends." We intended to do that, no matter how the others reacted. Rosalynn began listing names of people we hoped would help. Most of the time, we planned our trip by telephone, since we were 180 miles apart. We chose to go to Tallahassee first. It was close to Plains, and is Florida's state capital. We then planned to head toward Fort Walton Beach and Panama City and dip down the Gulf Coast toward Tampa. Then we would start north again through Dade City, Ocala, Gainesville, Lake City, and finally back home to Plains. We projected a two-week trip.

6

Florida, Here We Come

I TURNED into the Carter driveway April 13, 1975, eager to go to Florida. Both Rosalynn and I believed in Jimmy Carter, and Florida was the key to the Southern states' primaries.

Though we had planned carefully, there were a few last-minute preparations and arrangements that had to be tended to after I arrived in Plains. We packed all of our clothes and campaign supplies into Rosalynn's beige Chevrolet. Not knowing what to expect on the two-week excursion, we took several suitcases each, clothes in garment bags, plenty of makeup, and other personal items—even the coffee pot. Can you believe that old coffee pot never made it out of the car, much less saw any service? As for the clothes, only a few items were ever worn. There was no time for leisurely morning coffee or for changing clothes during the day. We didn't make that mistake again. As a result of that first campaign trip to Florida, we became quite proficient at packing.

Since the trunk was full of our belongings, we filled the backseat with the campaign materials that were available in those early days. Jimmy received excellent press in his preliminary ventures in Iowa in March of 1975, so we had several boxes containing hundreds of copies of one particularly favorable editorial. In addition, we had a one-page biography; some campaign brochures; pages from a 1974 Florida political almanac, giving background census, districts, and a list of Democratic Party chairpersons; almost primitive position papers on a variety of subjects; and *nine* bumper stickers. Nine bumper stickers for the entire state of Florida. No more were available.

To say the least, the campaign materials were not well organized. In fact, they weren't organized at all. There was no such thing as packets of materials; consequently, while one of us drove, the other arranged the items into some semblance of order and stuffed them into manageable units. When stuffing became too tedious, we switched places. We managed to get enough packets ready for the next stop, gave away the material, got back into the car, and stuffed some more. All the way to Tallahassee, we drove and stuffed and talked and planned.

Occasionally as we rode, we talked about the "butterflies." For us, the butterflies were symbolic yet very real fears that Rosalynn experienced as she ventured into the national political campaign arena. It is true that Rosalynn is basically a private person and has her share of inhibitions, but she knew these butterflies simply had to go, when push came to shove —when the "Go make friends" campaign got underway.

*   *   *   *

Through the years of their marriage, Rosalynn had courageously challenged various inhibitions. From their earliest days together, Jimmy recognized her ability to accomplish anything she wanted or needed to do, and he knew how to inspire confidence in her ability to set her sights on achieving these goals.

When they took on the struggling Carter family business, Jimmy became the managing director and Rosalynn the bookkeeper. She knew little about farming, peanuts, and bookkeeping, but the job needed to be done, money was not available to hire a professional, Jimmy said she could do it, and she *wanted* to do it, so that was that. As the years went by, Rosalynn became the professional they needed. She developed such skill in agribusiness that when Jack Carter opened the Gordon County Grain Company in Calhoun, dealing in soybeans and corn, he asked Rosalynn to come help him. Rosalynn showed Vickie Spence, wife of Charles, one of Jack's partners, how to set up the books and keep records.

Rosalynn became so proficient as a comptroller that at one point, she planned to take the Certified Public Accountant examination. When the Carters moved to Atlanta, it became necessary to hire a local CPA to keep their business and personal finances in order. She was startled when the accountant's first bill arrived. "To think," she declared, "I've been worth *that* much all these years. Jimmy owes me lots of money!"

This dimension of their relationship, where Jimmy has been the encouragement and inspiration to develop her natural abilities, has extended itself to other areas of their lives.

Years later, Rosalynn, as First Lady, would easily and graciously face a hostile crowd of petitioners at the gate of the White House, hear their complaints, tolerate some heckling from the back of the crowd, thank them for their interest, and walk quickly back into the White House with hardly a flutter of the old butterflies.

I am intrigued by the self-improvement courses Rosalynn and Jimmy have taken through the years. While in Plains, she took courses at nearby Georgia Southwestern College in Americus. One was a modified speed-reading course; another she enjoyed was a course on the "Basic Issues of Life," featuring great literary writers. She and Jimmy studied *Books on the Great Masters* and continue their interest in art. Rosalynn cites a teacher in Plains who sparked her interest in art by displaying great works and requiring students to identify them. This same teacher repeated the procedure with great pieces of music, playing the records and asking the students to name the composers. Rosalynn admits that she and the other students weren't anxious to learn that information, but now her store of knowledge is appreciated, and she wants the same basic inspiration for Amy.

Rosalynn also has studied square dancing, ballroom dancing, piano, Spanish, and flower arranging.

Someone may ask, "Why has she spent so much time with all these pursuits?" The answer, from either Rosalynn or Jimmy, always is, "We like to learn. It's fun. We enjoy studying together."

Rosalynn's intense drive to better herself in various fields of study and to sharpen her mind and exercise her talents has proved invaluable in the political arena. The butterflies have given way to the bold affirmations of her family's "You can do it."

As her confidence increased and her world expanded, she became the eyes and ears for Jimmy in Georgia, and later throughout the nation, as we campaigned together. In a crowd, with people milling and conversation cascading around her, she can quickly make judgments on what deserves or demands action, often with far-reaching results.

In May, 1974, Bill Gunter was seeking a Law Day speaker for the University of Georgia. He wanted the governor but found out through an aide that Jimmy already had an engagement. At a party for newspaper editors, Bill talked with Rosalynn, explained the situation, and described the importance of this day to the students. The next day, Jimmy's secretary called Bill, to say the governor could come. This chain of events resulted in Jimmy Carter's Law Day speech, which was made known internationally by reporter and author Hunter Thompson. Thompson came to Athens that day to cover another speaker, Ted Kennedy, but went away with a recording of the Georgia governor's speech. He was so impressed by the Carter statement he played it far and near, giving credibility to Jimmy Carter.

As Rosalynn was Jimmy's eyes and ears on the campaign trail, I found myself providing a similar service for her. While Rosalynn described Jimmy Carter to one group of people in a room or courthouse, I talked with others who wanted to ask questions about the Carters, to make suggestions, or to align themselves with the campaign. Together, Rosalynn and I discussed the ideas, questions, and offers of help that were put to us, acting immediately on some and deferring others. But we always filed away what we heard and who we met, knowing full well that everyone was important to the campaign.

                    *   *   *   *

Before we embarked on our first Florida trip, we worked out housing plans. Since we wanted to meet people, to be with them and know them, to hear their problems and share their dreams, we decided to stay in private homes wherever possible. This was one of the best decisions of the campaign. Eventually, the system of staying with people became institutionalized into what we called "Carter Innkeepers."

Al and Shirley Seckinger of Tampa were the first to be given the title Innkeeper. Jimmy and Al grew up together in Plains, where Al's father was pastor of the Lutheran Church. Through the years, the men, both engineers, church workers, and political activists, had maintained their friendship. Shirley, a registered pharmacist, works one day a week at her profession, while maintaining a very orderly household.

Into this carefully orchestrated life-style came crashing dozens of Carter campaign workers over a period of nineteen months. Rosalynn and I were the first to stay in the Seckingers' house, but before it was all over, practically the entire campaign entourage benefited from Al and Shirley's hospitality. Jack and Judy, Chip and Caron, Jeff and Annette, and many others spent time in the Seckinger Inn. With unflagging good humor, Al and Shirley furnished bed and board, provided a phone-answering service and campaign checkpoint, loaned money to broke young campaign workers, forwarded clothes that had been left hanging in closets, and did just about anything else imaginable to help energetic campaign workers do their thing for Jimmy Carter.

Along the way, as Rosalynn and I visited with the hosts and their families, she would say, "We'll entertain you at the White House someday." Rosalynn and I believed it, and gradually we sensed many new friends believed it, too. You can imagine the jubilation and satisfaction many of the Innkeepers felt when, on the Friday after Jimmy's inauguration, all Innkeepers were invited to the White House to be thanked by the new First Family and to receive an engraved copper plaque stating: "A member of the Jimmy Carter family stayed in this house during the 1976 campaign."

The first night of our initial campaign trip, we landed in Tallahassee. Rosalynn and I stayed with Doug and Judi Henderson, a young couple Beverly and I met at Emory University Hospital in Atlanta. After completing Doug's medical work, the Hendersons moved to Tallahassee to establish a practice. One phone call to the Hendersons assured us of reservations in their home.

For our first official reception, we suggested inviting approximately 30 to 50 people, but our hostess, Eleanor Ketchum, mailed out 400 invitations, and 308 people came to her home!

Rosalynn's charm, unpretentiousness, and intelligence were appealing. Those at that first coffee seemed drawn to her and consequently became interested in her candidate.

An added benefit of this reception became evident when Mrs. Pat Miller, a member of the Democratic Party Committee for the Tallahas-

see area, introduced herself to Rosalynn and asked, "Whose idea was it
to invite Democratic Party Committee members to this coffee?"

Not sure what Mrs. Miller had in mind, Rosalynn replied, "It was
mine. It seemed the natural thing to do. You're the leaders in the Democratic Party, and Jimmy is asking the Democratic Party to nominate
him."

Mrs. Miller answered, "This is the first time we have been invited to
anything like this. Candidates have come and gone but have never called
on us. I'm going to help you." Right on the spot, Mrs. Miller gave us
a list of Democrats in other parts of the Florida panhandle. This scenario
was repeated over and over again. The obvious people, the grass-roots
leaders, had been overlooked for years. Once they were included and felt
needed by the Carter team, they worked to help nominate Jimmy.

The overwhelming response that spring morning at this first official
campaign event reinforced our confidence in the timing of Jimmy's
candidacy and its immense potential for success. Rosalynn's effectiveness
as a solo campaigner was established, and it was apparent that the
people-to-people format used in the Georgia governor's race would be
effective in a national effort.

One of my favorite hobbies is antiquing. To me, campaigning has all
the anticipation and excitement of a visit to a big antique show. You are
going to see articles you've not seen before, with the possibility of finding
a real bargain, of getting just what you've been looking for. Campaigning
in a new territory, meeting new people, and influencing voters to support
your candidate gives me the same thrill. Rosalynn and I attacked our
campaigning with great enthusiasm and anticipation.

Judy still chuckles when she says that we slid in and out of automobiles so much that the lining of our coats sagged below the hemline and
we walked so much we regularly wore holes in the toes of our hose.

In the opening days of our efforts, we fell into a pattern that generally
held for the duration of the campaign. Rosalynn did most of the handshaking and talking, while I handed out brochures and wrote down the
names and addresses of those we met. To save time and to avoid confusion, we often didn't give my name. Sometimes people mistook me for
Rosalynn, because we are about the same height and size, and most
people did not know either of us. Our intent throughout the campaign
was to leave only one name in the minds of the people—Jimmy Carter.

Inevitably, however, someone would come over to me while the crowds swirled around Rosalynn and ask hesitantly, "And who are you?"

Recently, during a visit to the White House, I saw Rosalynn greeting a crowd at the gate. While she talked with the group, I watched. Very shyly, a little boy walked over, looked me straight in the eye, asking, "And who are *you* ?" All of our friends erupted with laughter.

At the end of the campaign day, Rosalynn gave me any new information she wanted filed. We discussed the day's events, making notes and assessments. Often after Rosalynn went to bed and fell asleep, I stayed up, making notes and indicating important items for future contacts. Usually at night the bedroom and bathroom were the only rooms where I felt I would not disturb our hosts. I would move to the bathroom for these late-night sessions, with my little three-by-five-inch cards spread around me. As I described our procedure to a friend, she said, "Why did Rosalynn go to bed so early? Did she find the pressures of the crowd too much?" Crowds? What crowds? In those days, we were begging for crowds. Rosalynn just required more sleep than I did.

Rooming together was easy for us, because our personal habits were different. Rosalynn washed her hair at night and slept with it wet. She took her bath in the morning and rolled her hair on hot curlers. I took my bath at night but washed my hair in the morning and just let it dry. We always put out our next day's clothes, packing all the others. This expedited our leaving the next morning. Rosalynn hated being late for anything, and we rarely were!

Each new day of our first foray into Florida honed our sense of organization, strengthened our self-confidence, and deepened our appreciation for the people. Rosalynn eventually spent at least seventy-five days campaigning in Florida. I believe these opening days were most crucial in shaping Rosalynn into a very successful spokeswoman for Jimmy's presidential campaign.

7

Courthouses and Cow Barns

"IF THERE IS ONE thing I have learned by being in the White House," Rosalynn said, "it's that everyone is important. People need us, and we need them. Being here is a humbling experience, when we look at all the people who helped us get here."

There's no doubt about it: Rosalynn and Jimmy Carter are "of the people." They just don't have the elitist mentality. This has something to do with the pattern she and I developed as we began our campaigning for the Carter presidency in 1975.

Few people have even heard of Quincy, a small county seat ten miles from Tallahassee in the Florida panhandle. No one in that town knew that Rosalynn and I were coming. And had they known, it would have created little interest. This was still in the days of "Jimmy who?"

We did not know a single person in Quincy, but that didn't matter. We knew where to start: the county courthouse. Some have asked why we picked the courthouse. Both Rosalynn and I recognized the strategic position of the Clerk of the Court in most counties. He or she is responsible for a significant part of the county's business. Clerks usually remain in office for several terms. We reasoned that the clerk could provide political information about the county, as well as introduce us to other officials in the courthouse. We went to Quincy in early 1975—more than a year before the presidential primary. We felt that politically sensitive courthouse officials would already be on the alert for local and national candidates. We wanted them to know Jimmy's name and to know him as a serious candidate.

We also knew that by reaching the people in the courthouse, our story would spread throughout the county. People would see us. Employees would talk about us. Later in the day, in the restaurants, over supper tables, in barber shops or beauty parlors, people would mention our coming. People would tell each other at church or share our news with visiting relatives. After all, the wife of a presidential candidate had never come to these small towns in Florida before.

We imagined this conversation: "The funniest thing happened at the courthouse today. I looked up from the water cooler, and here came two women. One said, 'Good morning. I'm Mrs. Jimmy Carter, and my husband is running for president.' Before I could say 'President of what?' this Mrs. Carter smiled and said, 'President of the United States, and I want you to be interested in him.' Mrs. Carter gave me a brochure, shook my hand, talked with me for a minute, and then moved on up the hall. Whoever heard of Jimmy Carter? And whoever heard of anyone campaigning for President of the United States in the courthouse in Quincy, Florida?"

We agreed that the story should echo for days. Most important, Rosalynn's visit would be remembered at primary-election time, when Jimmy Carter would be better known.

Courthouses are not hard to find. After parking at the one in Quincy, we gathered up brochures and started inside, to find the clerk's office. Before we entered the building, Rosalynn looked at me and said, "Do you realize what we're doing? Can you *believe* it?" I did and she did. We believed, took a deep breath, and went inside.

An attractive lady met us at the counter in the clerk's office, identifying herself as the clerk's wife, Douglas Baur, (yes, *Douglas—she*). We talked with her for several minutes. She became openly enthusiastic. Minutes later, she was taking us in and out of all the county offices. We talked, laughed, handed out materials, shook hands, mentioned Jimmy's achievements as governor of Georgia, told them of his goals, and concluded by asking them to be interested in his campaign.

That didn't end our trip. After we had gone through all the offices, Mrs. Baur took us to the county commissioner's meeting. Rosalynn and I met the entire group of county officials, representing each section of the county, in one fell swoop. Rosalynn introduced herself and, for the fiftieth time that day, told why she had come to Quincy. They smiled, asked a few questions, and several of them said, "We'll be keeping our eyes on Jimmy Carter from now on." Rosalynn thanked them, and we left.

We had spent almost the entire morning there. We had to reach Bonifay, about a twenty minute drive, for a twelve o'clock luncheon.

We rushed out of Quincy, hurrying as fast as we could. We did not want to keep the people of Bonifay waiting. Shortly after our trip to Quincy, we learned how to make quick getaways. First, we had a second set of car keys made. No matter who was driving, each unlocked her own door. That meant we didn't have to waste precious seconds while the driver unlocked her door, got in, reached across, and unlocked the passenger's door. Second, we worked out the seat-belt problem. The car, a Chevrolet, would not start unless the passenger's seat belt was fastened, too. So the passenger would rise off her seat while the driver started the car. Then, as we drove off, the passenger could sit back down and fasten her safety belt. It may have looked strange, but it seemed to save time!

It may also seem silly to some that we worried about losing those few seconds, but it was because we wanted to make the best use of our time, to get to more places to meet more people. Then, too, Rosalynn once said, "I don't like to be kept waiting, myself. Why should I make others wait for me?" That kind of sensitivity is part of what makes Rosalynn Carter the person she is.

We arrived in Bonifay on time. Harvey Etheridge, a local radio personality, met us, introduced us to the group of city and county officials and civic leaders, then we enjoyed a Dutch luncheon with them. Harvey had asked to interview Rosalynn immediately after lunch but had made one stipulation: "Your statements should not be political."

Rosalynn and I both wondered how he could interview her, the wife of a presidential candidate traveling on a campaign trip, and still not ask anything political.

He posed several questions. She answered quietly and, I felt, with great poise. After a few minutes, he must have changed his mind about the nonpolitical stipulation. "Is your husband *really* a serious candidate for the presidency?"

"Yes, he is," she said, and then explained why. I watched his face and saw that she had captivated him. He dropped his defenses, and the interview seemed to flow smoothly. Just before we left, he said, "We're going to have an all-night gospel sing here. We'd like to have Jimmy Carter, himself, come that night."

Harvey Etheridge's invitation was only the first of many to come as a result of our trip. We made the initial contact, paving the way for bigger, better events for Jimmy.

That same afternoon we drove to Chipley, county seat of Washington County, Florida. In that lovely, tree-shaded town, we took part in three events. We moved through the courthouse, much as we had done in Quincy. We participated in an afternoon tea, and following that, we went to a cow sale. Yes, that's right, a cow sale!

When we reached Chipley's courthouse, instead of being tired from an already busy day, Rosalynn seemed infused with new energy. She looked more confident and said, "I've already done this once." She could do it again, as often as necessary. This time she did not hesitate as we got out of the car and headed up the steps of the charming, old building. We found the clerk's office, received a warm reception, and minutes later walked up and down the corridors, meeting people and saying, "We'd like you to be interested in Jimmy Carter's campaign."

The invitation to tea came about in an unusual way, but by then, everything was beginning to happen in unusual ways. As a state senator, my husband had two secretaries, Judy Gilbert and Trisha Lee, both of whom had once lived in this area. They still had friends and contacts in the panhandle. When they heard about our plans to visit Florida, they wanted to help. Judy called her friend, Jude Gibson, who was active in Chipley civic affairs. After telling her of our coming visit, Judy asked for help. Without hesitating, Mrs. Gibson volunteered to have a tea in her home. "Chipley loves to have parties, whatever the occasion. We'll invite everybody, and we'll have it late in the afternoon, so the teachers can come."

What may have seemed to be only a social event established a pattern that was repeated again and again over the country. Friends and neighbors helped the hostess with her party. They brought some of the refreshments, helped ready the house, and came to meet the guest of honor. When the group gathered, Rosalynn spoke to them, in her informal way. She told them of Jimmy's accomplishments as governor of Georgia and why he would make a good president. She told them what we were doing and how they could be involved. As she talked, I watched their reactions. The interest she kindled was quite visible. Often a friendly neighbor said confidentially to me, "I just came so my friend would have some people here. But now I want to help!"

After the tea, at Jude Gibson's suggestion, we went to Chipley's Tuesday-evening cow sale.

Visiting a cow sale probably does not sound like much, to city people. But as small-town people, we understood. The weekly Chipley cattle sale, like hundreds of cow sales in rural America, draws farmers and ranchers, merchants and beef brokers from the entire area. Truck farmers haul in produce, which they sell off the backs of their pickup trucks and stake-bodied vehicles. A happy spirit always seems to pervade a cattle sale. It has a semblance of Old World markets, where neighbors and friends gather to trade gossip, exchange ideas, and pass on tales of current happenings. Rosalynn and I were no strangers to cattle sales; over the years, we had attended many such events.

Mrs. Gibson said, "Find Buddy Neal. He's the man to see." She told us that he had been president of the Cattlemen's Association of Florida. He lived in the Chipley community, owned the barn, ran the sale, and was probably the most influential person there.

We parked between two trucks, collected some brochures, and walked into the barn. The auctioneer was already bawling out his mysterious spiel over the cows. We asked a couple of people where we could find Buddy, and finally someone pointed him out.

We walked over and introduced ourselves. In a quiet voice, despite all the noise and bustle around us, she explained why we had come and that Mrs. Gibson had told us to contact him.

"Glad to meet you, ladies," he said, asking us to sit down beside him while the sales continued. Not knowing what else to do, we sat down. I gave Rosalynn a quick glance, trying to ask, "What now?"

She understood, and her wordless communication said, "Wait. It will work itself out!" Obviously, Buddy Neal did not know what to do with us.

Rosalynn commented about the cow up for auction. We chatted about the barn and the weather. Rosalynn and I soon grew restless. I began fidgeting, not sure what we ought to do. Hundreds of people were milling around outside. We wanted to tell them about Jimmy Carter, and we were just sitting there.

After what we felt was an appropriate amount of time, Rosalynn got up and said, "It was nice to meet you, Mr. Neal. Please excuse us." Although our new acquaintance did not know what to do, she did. We moved out toward the crowd. Just as we had done in the courthouse, we went up to people, introduced ourselves, and told them about Jimmy's desire to become the Democratic nominee. Everyone responded warmly and accepted the literature we offered.

A few minutes later, I turned around, and there was Buddy Neal. He was looking for us. He smiled, but I felt he was slightly embarrassed. He said, "Ladies, I apologize. When you came in here announcing that you were campaigning for Jimmy Carter for President of the United States, I was so surprised I didn't know what to do. Please come back inside and let me introduce you to all these folks. And, Mrs. Carter, if you want to say something to the crowd, please feel free to do so."

He led us to the auctioneer's stand and raised his hand. The auctioneer stopped, and Buddy Neal introduced Rosalynn. The auctioneer had just described a cow as one of the most beautiful ones he had ever auctioned. Before he had a chance to get the first bid, Rosalynn was introduced. She stood up, thanked Mr. Neal, his friends, and the community. She spoke briefly about her favorite subject, Jimmy Carter. Then she stepped down.

The people applauded warmly as she walked away. I looked back as the auctioneer took his place. It took him a few seconds to get back to the cow, but he began right where he had left off.

Leaving the building, we stopped and spoke to everyone we met. We urged them to become interested in Jimmy. Before getting to the car, we discussed politics with the produce farmers and their customers around their trucks. We talked, and we listened until it was quite dark.

Driving away toward Crestview in the warm Florida night, we experienced our first real sense of accomplishment. Our positive feeling that Jimmy was on his way to the White House was affirmed. Our belief in what we were doing was as strong at the end of that second day of campaigning as it was on the eve of the Democratic Convention fourteen months later!

I did not keep count, but in those two weeks, we must have visited at least a dozen courthouses or city halls. But that was the only cow barn!

The courthouse visits provided a kaleidoscope of unforgettable personal and political experiences.

I remember we were somewhat hesitant when we visited in Tampa. We parked our campaign car and turned our minds toward repeating the courthouse experiences from the early part of the week. But the Hillsborough County Courthouse in Tampa was different from the others. We saw a huge, modern office building. As we entered, there was a receptionist in the lobby. We looked at each other, and Rosalynn charged right ahead. She may have been nervous, but she would not let that stop her.

She told the receptionist why we had come and what we wanted to do. The woman explained that we would have to obtain permission from the clerk. I felt Rosalynn tighten up slightly, but she did not hesitate. "I would like to meet the clerk."

The receptionist sent us to James Taylor. He listened, left the work he was obviously involved in when we came to his office, and took us through the building. More than 200 people worked in the courthouse, and he went through every office, introducing Rosalynn.

As we left the courthouse, Rosalynn said, "I can tell you now—I almost didn't go in there. I was scared. The building was so huge. I almost rebelled. But James Taylor made us feel at home, and I'm glad we did it."

"Rosalynn," I answered, "you were wonderful. You showed such poise, no one would have known about those butterflies."

"Well, thank you for going with me. I wouldn't have done it without you."

As I walked along, I felt glad to be traveling with her. She had thanked me—not just then, but countless times.

That's part of the reason people feel comfortable around Rosalynn. She's sensitive to others. She appreciates their helpfulness and tells them. I've seen her in almost every kind of situation. She has often won people over who came prepared to dislike her. She always handles herself well, even with people who strongly disagree with her or Jimmy, treating friend or political enemy alike.

Visiting courthouses provided us with more than an opportunity to meet people. We also picked up information about people in the state. We realized that voters in Florida, although still fond of George Wallace, were beginning to move away from him. The crippling effect of the assassin's bullet, linked with changing times, had persuaded many Floridians that George Wallace's day had come and gone. They felt that Wallace could not win nationally, and they wanted a winner. They were looking for a new political leader. Carter was still too new on the scene for the people of north Florida to make commitments, but they promised to watch his campaign. We believed from the beginning that Jimmy had more than a fighting chance to carry the Sunshine State. The more we talked to people, the more convinced we became of eventual victory here.

As we traveled, we recognized the futility of saying, "We want you to vote for Jimmy Carter." The primary was a year away, and the general election eighteen months ahead. The statement both Rosalynn and I used was simply, "We want you to be interested in Jimmy Carter." At that point, we could ask for nothing more, and we liked the sound of what we were saying. We also knew that the day would come when we could use the word *vote,* and we had already prepared the way for that.

Rosalynn and I were not the only Carter people who visited courthouses. Most of those on the road did, too. They all had their own favorite courthouse story. Jack Carter's story illustrates how everything was beginning to fit into place.

Part of Jack's early strategy was to visit counties where they had no Carter chairman. He would look for someone to fill that position. Usually he visited the courthouse, met people, and often found the right person. During one particularly long day of courthouse campaigning, he came to a small county in Florida that had no county chairman. After going through the courthouse, meeting a number of people—most of them responsive—Jack still did not feel he had found the right person.

He was not sure what to do next. He hated to leave without knowing he had assigned that responsibility. Leaving the courthouse, he sat down on the steps, trying to decide what to do.

A young lawyer came up. In typical small-town fashion, he began a conversation by introducing himself. Jack explained why he had come, and the lawyer expressed interest. Jack needed a phone, so he asked where he could find one. "Come on over to my office and use mine," the lawyer said.

As the two walked over and their conversation continued, Jack became convinced he had found the person he was looking for. He stopped and said, "Would you like to become the Carter campaign chairperson for your county?"

"I sure would," the lawyer replied.

This brand of Carter luck, combined with hard work and strategy, brought the campaign the friends and support we were seeking. It emphasized to us that no matter how hard we planned or how fervently we worked, we could not accomplish anything without people. Finding the key person in each community made the difference.

In November, 1979, I saw these words on a chalkboard in an Iowa campaign headquarters:

> We can spend until we empty our treasuries, and we may summon all the wonders of science, but we can succeed only if we tap our greatest resource—AMERICA'S PEOPLE.
>
> Jimmy Carter

Rosalynn and I moved from courthouse to courthouse. We spread the name of Jimmy Carter with our appearances, our brochures, and our nine bumper stickers. But mostly we met people. And here we learned to appreciate human beings as never before. We moved among the people. We learned their dreams, their frustrations, and their needs. All the while, Rosalynn was growing. She seemed to mature each day, as I watched a more confident Rosalynn emerge.

Someone commented on her growing political sophistication. She replied, "I suppose my political growth comes from my ability to identify with people. When I was a child, my mother made my clothes, my father drove a school bus. I knew what it was like not to have money.

"When I married Jimmy, we traveled a lot, moving to the Northeast and then to Hawaii, where Chip, our second son, was born. I knew what it was like to be uprooted and to make new friends. When we moved back to Plains, I went to work in the warehouse. I knew what it was like to have a job. When the business became successful, I knew what it was to have a more secure feeling about money. When Jimmy entered politics, I knew what it was like to experience both defeat and victory. In all areas of life, I identify with the people. As I have listened to them and talked with them, I can understand."

*   *   *   *

She does understand. Even more than understanding, she has done something about it. For example, I've watched her growing concern with the following:

Education.   She has been an advocate of better education and a friend of teachers for as long as I have known her. She and Jimmy showed their concern for education as early as the 1960s, when Jimmy served on the Sumter County school board. They never lost that concern, even when they moved from local to state politics.

Two landmarks in education came about because of the Carters' backing. One was the Governor's Honors Program, mentioned previously. Later, as president, Jimmy established the Department of Education as a separate unit, dissolving its relationship with the Department of Health and Welfare.

Officials of the National Education Association (NEA) clearly recognized the Carters' concern for quality education. One of them said, at an NEA banquet in 1979: "Education is the easiest area to make promises in. It's also the easiest to forget when the going gets rough." Then he quickly added, "But not so with Jimmy and Rosalynn Carter as President and First Lady. After their commitment to education, they set a course and stayed firm."

In October, 1979, at the White House, President and Mrs. Carter were congratulating the NEA board of directors because of the newly established Department of Education. Jimmy added, with that characteristic twinkle in his blue eyes, "That passed with an overwhelming majority of two."

Loud applause broke out. They clapped for the President and First Lady, who had persisted when failure seemed certain. They were also clapping for themselves, as they enjoyed their long-sought autonomy.

At the celebration banquet, when Shirley Hufstedler was sworn in as the first Secretary of the Department of Education, she praised the Carters for making "A fifty-eight-year pursuit a reality."

Many educators acknowledge Rosalynn's continued quest for quality education. Atlanta's Bill Milliken, president of Cities in Schools, said recently, "I was at the capital when Governor Carter officially announced his candidacy for president. Both Governor and Mrs. Carter had contributed time and money to our program of urban education, even though I had not seen them for several months. As I turned to leave the press conference, I saw Mrs. Carter and nodded to her.

"She came over to me and asked me how the program was going. Hardly before I knew what was happening, she invited me to supper *that night*. We talked until three in the morning about the poor, ineffective urban schools and what we needed to do to correct those deplorable conditions. I don't think she was politely doing the work of a governor's wife. She listened, asked pertinent questions, and made perceptive comments. One of the first innovations President Carter announced after he took office was a program that implemented the work of Cities in Schools. Thanks to Mrs. Carter, the White House is keeping in close contact with the Cities in Schools programs."

The elderly.   Rosalynn understands the plight of senior citizens. She has a vivid picture of an aged aunt, needlessly rocking away the last years of her life because society said she was no longer productive. She anxiously watched her mother, Miss Allie, come to retirement age after decades of useful work and community service.

From the days in the governor's mansion, Rosalynn recognized the value of older Americans as full participants in our country. She frequently emphasized this and made special efforts to meet and talk with the elderly during the campaign.

My own parents had retired south of Tampa, in Sun City Center, a retirement community. Most in this community are active in civic club and churches.

Politically, many of the residents were longtime Republicans from various parts of the country. Nevertheless, mother invited her friends to a tea, to meet Rosalynn and to learn about Jimmy. When they left that afternoon, all of them were interested in Jimmy and promised to consider supporting him.

Later, as those same people visited relatives and friends in other states, they told others about Jimmy and Rosalynn. We learned that many of them reregistered as Democrats to vote for Jimmy!

The handicapped.   At a ceremony in the East Room of the White House in July, 1979, the media gave good coverage to the issuing of a commemorative stamp honoring the Special Olympics for the Handicapped. Just before she unveiled the painting from which the stamp had been copied, Eunice Shriver told the assembled people:

> Mrs. Carter, Postmaster Bolger, members of Congress, ambassadors, Special Olympians, parents, friends. . . .
> This is a fantastic day for Special Olympics. My only regret is that my parents could not be here. For it was they who gave to my sister Rosemary the love, the pride, the accomplishment that are the very core of Special Olympics. It was they who taught us to stand together, to work together, to make the most out of the experience of having a special child in our family. And now this beautiful postage stamp will say to families everywhere, "Have hope and belief in your special children. They are respected; they are welcomed by the nation and by the world."
> I would like to add a very personal comment. Although Mrs. Carter has already told you of her point of view, I would like to tell what it's been like for those of us who have worked with her. In 1972, when Special Olympics was very young and not a bit prominent, the third international games were taking place in Los Angeles. One governor's wife arrived—one. It was Mrs. Jimmy Carter, and she came as a volunteer. She marched in the parade, she lived in the dormitory, and she chaperoned her state's athletes.
> Four years later, another international came. That same governor's wife—again the only one—was there. Again she marched in the parade, again she lived in the dormitory, again she chaperoned the Georgia delegation, gave the medals, gave the awards, and stayed the whole time.
> Mrs. Carter, your husband urged us, in a speech two nights ago, to make sacrifices. He called upon us for courage; he has asked us for commitment. If he is looking for an example for this country, he need look no further than you.

Thunderous applause erupted and swept over the audience. A surprised and visibly embarrassed First Lady tried to smile. Rosalynn told me later, "I went to the Special Olympics because it's something I believe in. I didn't go to be political." People know hers is not a skin-deep concern for the handicapped of our nation. In fact, Rosalynn believes that being named honorary chairperson of the Commission on Mental Health is the most important responsibility she has had since becoming the First Lady.

Rosalynn cares about people of all ages—in all places—from courthouses to cow barns.

Pre-wedding party for Jack and Judy, October, 1971, in Atlanta.
Seated: Rosalynn Carter, Edna Langford. *Standing, left to right:*
Chip Carter, Jeff Carter, Jack Carter, Judy Langford, Governor
Jimmy Carter, Beth Russell, Jim Langford, J. Beverly Langford.

Edna Langford and Rosalynn Carter in the governor's mansion in Atlanta, Georgia, during a reception for Betty Ford, April, 1974. *Below:* Rosalynn and Edna Langford, the night of the Pennsylvania primary, April, 1976 (© 1976 Mikki Ehrenfeld).

A 1976 family portrait. *From front to back:* Amy, Rosalynn, Jimmy, Annette, Jeff, Chip, Caron, Jason, Jack, Judy (© 1976 Charles M. Rafshoon).

Beverly Langford presenting Jimmy with a watch from the Seventh Congressional District Carter Campaign Committee in summer, 1970, during the campaign for Georgia governor. The committee gave Jimmy the watch when they found he didn't have one. *Below:* The inaugural parade, January 20, 1977. Rosalynn is wearing the blue teal coat and dress (White House photo).

Inauguration Day, 1977. *Left to right:* Judy Langford Carter, Jason Carter (on Jack's shoulders), President Carter, Amy, Chip and Caron Carter, Rosalynn, Annette and Jeff Carter (White House photo). *Right:* Amy and Rosalynn at the inaugural ball. Rosalynn is wearing her "old" dress (White House photo).

Amy and Rosalynn in Africa, April, 1978 (White House photo). *Left:* Rosalynn and Edna on Air Force One on the way to Costa Rica for the inauguration of President Rodrigo Carozo, May, 1978 (White House photo).

Rosalynn fishing in the Grand Tetons of Wyoming, August, 1978 (White House photo). *Below:* Rosalynn and Jimmy on a Salmon River, Idaho, raft trip, August 22, 1978 (White House photo).

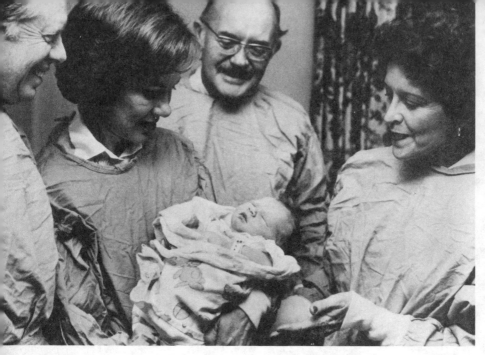

Jimmy, Rosalynn, Beverly Langford, Edna Langford with Sarah
Rosemary Carter, born December 19, 1978 (White House photo).
Below: Judy, Jason, and Jack Carter at the White House for the
signing of the Israeli-Egyptian peace treaty in March, 1979. Annette
Carter is in the background (White House photo).

Rosalynn and Jimmy on their daily run, White House south lawn, March, 1979 (White House photo).

Rosalynn and Jimmy outside the old Executive Office Building, May, 1979 (White House photo). *Below:* Rosalynn in her room at the White House, 1979 (White House photo).

Rosalynn saying good-bye to Jimmy as he leaves the White House south lawn in August, 1979 (White House photo). *Below:* Rosalynn meets Pope John Paul II as he arrives in Boston, October 1, 1979 (White House photo).

Rosalynn enjoying a 1979 Columbus Day Parade (White House photo). *Right:* Rosalynn meeting the press at a Cambodian refugee camp in Thailand, November, 1979 (White House photo).

Rosalynn with Cambodian child in a Thailand refugee camp, November, 1979 (White House photo). *Below:* Rosalynn speaks at the December 7, 1979 announcement of Jimmy's presidential candidacy (© 1979 Audley Tucker).

Rosalynn with Sarah Rosemary Carter in the State Dining Room, December 17, 1979. The room is decorated for the state dinner given for Margaret Thatcher, prime minister of England (White House photo).

Opposite page: State dinner for Prime Minister Margaret Thatcher, Green Room of the White House. *Left to right:* Prime Minister Thatcher, Edna Langford, Miss Allie Smith (Rosalynn's mother), President Carter, Rosalynn Carter (White House photo). *Bottom:* Sarah's first birthday, in the White House solarium. *Foreground:* Jason and Sarah Carter. *Second row:* Rosalynn, Amy, Judy. *Back:* Gay Gunter, Edna Langford, James Carter, held by Ann Smith, Rosalynn's niece (White House photo).

Lucie Langford worked on Jimmy Carter's campaign staff during the 1976 primaries. *Below:* Jim and Barbara Mauldin Langford, married May, 1980.

8

Meeting the Media

ROSALYNN SMITH CARTER stood on the red carpet at Boston's Logan International Airport to welcome Pope John Paul II to our country. She walked to the high speaker's platform, the lone female in a small contingent of distinguished clergymen.

Millions around the world watched that historic event via satellite TV. Flashes exploded, tape recorders whirred, and television cameras panned, as the crowds moved in closer to hear the resonant voice of the pontiff. They also strained to hear the small, gentle voice of Rosalynn Carter. It seemed as if the gusty Boston winds fanned the air of expectancy we all felt. She stood there, in a smart, black suit and a black velveteen cloche, to greet His Holiness in the name of the President of the United States and the American people. And why not? She is the First Lady. Yet I remember when people asked "Mrs. Who?"

Rosalynn Smith Carter's face has appeared on the covers of *Newsweek, People, Dossier, Time, Atlanta Journal, Constitution Magazine, U.S. News & World Report, The New York Times* sunday magazine, and inside other magazines. Everyone knows this energetic and beautiful woman. But I remember when no one wanted to take her picture.

All that has changed. She went from the obscurity of being a farmer's wife in south Georgia to becoming the most recognized woman in the world. She has matured as a person. She has grown as a political strategist. But she has not changed significantly from the first day I met her and we became friends.

Although she is as familiar to the public as any movie star, few people know the real Rosalynn Carter.

Recently my phone rang. The cheery voice said, "Mrs. Langford, I am doing a feature story about Rosalynn Carter. What can you tell me about her?" Another reporter. I am no longer surprised, since this often happens. I try to answer the best I can, trying to select illustrative experiences from the years we have known each other.

While I have mentioned her sensitivity, her warmth, and her concern for people, Rosalynn is, and always has been, a private person. Because she has guarded this privacy, some have mistaken her attitude for coldness and standoffishness. Every time I hear people refer to her as the Steel Magnolia, I bristle. I keep thinking, *Oh, if only they knew her the way I do.* She is strong. She's a woman of deep convictions. When she has a purpose, nothing deters her, no matter how unpopular her actions appear. But she is not that unfeeling caricature the media has sometimes presented.

Because we are close friends, it is hard to be objective about her. Friendship has a way of cluttering up a person's point of view. Realizing this, I have tried many times to watch her as if I were a total outsider. Her candor and genuine humility always shine through.

Her appearance on Phil Donahue's television program was remarkable. She wore a beautiful white suit and an aqua blouse. She looked confident and petite, as the questions flew at her. With tact and good humor, she answered each question honestly. She avoided fielding the questions with obscure answers.

The live audience warmed to Rosalynn. Donahue did a fine job of letting viewers know the real First Lady. At one point, Phil pushed Rosalynn on a question. (The dozens of letters he received later revealed his viewers thought him too forceful.) His questions concerned the gasoline shortage in California in mid-1979. People often waited hours in long lines for gas. He asked, "Why is there a gas shortage in California? Is there really a national fuel shortage?"

Rosalynn replied simply, "If I knew those answers, I could solve the whole problem."

The audience enthusiastically applauded. She did not know, and she did not try to bluff. That is a picture of the real Rosalynn Carter.

* * * *

As I look back, it never occurred to us that she would one day be the focus of media attention. But even in early 1975, I knew she could handle any situation well.

In the beginning, we did not plan a "media image," as is often done when people groom themselves for public office. We embarked on a campaign venture to get the name of Jimmy Carter known. We approached each town with that one goal in mind.

When we first visited Florida, no one wanted to interview Rosalynn. We decided that since the media did not seek us, we would seek them. If they did not knock on our door, we had to bang on theirs. In each town, we made it a point to make at least two important stops: the local radio or television station and the local newspaper.

While nothing substitutes for personal, face-to-face encounter, it helped to have radio or television exposure first. People on the street or at receptions would say, "Hey, I saw you on television" or "I saw your picture in the newspaper" or "I recognize your voice from having heard it on the radio."

The only thing better than one appearance is two: one in person and one through the media. And, although it sounds silly to repeat that common expression, "You look just like your picture," nothing stirred that struggling candidate's wife more than to know people had heard her or seen her and remembered.

In searching for the local radio or television station, we sometimes had to ask for directions. If we were in a hurry (which we nearly always were), we used the dead-reckoning method. That is, we looked for the radio transmitter tower that stood taller than any building in town, and headed for it. Unfortunately, sometimes we wound up at the police station or at the location of a large ham-radio set. When it was possible, we made advance arrangements with a station. That did not happen often. Our usual method was to simply drop in.

Sometimes those pop-in visits threw the station personnel off guard.

We didn't want to be a problem or take up unnecessary time, yet we wanted them to interview Rosalynn. We developed a system. Rosalynn introduced herself: "I'm Mrs. Jimmy Carter. My husband is running for President of the United States." That opened the way for introductions and light conversation.

After a minute or two, I would say, "Wouldn't you like to interview Mrs. Carter? Her husband is going to be the next President of the United States."

Usually, the station personnel agreed to an interview. Since the primary was still a year away, these people often were at a loss as to what questions to pose. So we were prepared with a list of suggested questions. They often took the questions and made a tape with Rosalynn, perhaps to be used on more than one newscast. If the engineer also worked as newsman and sales manager and was out, we left a press packet of information with a note saying we hoped our visit would make the local news.

Rosalynn handled the interviews like a professional. She became more at ease with a question-and-answer format than giving a speech.

Her first call-in radio show was in Orlando, Florida, in May, 1975, during our second trip. Richard Swann, an Orlando lawyer, arranged for Rosalynn to be on Mike Miller's radio talk show from 10:00 P.M. to 12:00 midnight. After a busy day of campaigning, I did not want to subject her to two hours of something she had not done before. Richard did not want to cancel Rosalynn's appearance, so finally, after a brief shouting match between Richard and me in the hotel lobby, we compromised on a one-hour session from 10:00 P.M. to 11:00 P.M.

This turned out to be one of the best and most important events of that trip. The "Mike Miller Show," we discovered, was a very popular call-in, question-and-answer program (Rosalynn worked with him again recently in 1980, this time in Connecticut). All day prior to air time, the station advertised that "Mrs. Jimmy Carter" would be on the show. Rosalynn came into the studio, slipped her shoes off, and with elbows propped on the table, handled each call with the greatest of ease.

She gave each question serious thought before answering. She had made up her mind that she would not try to reply to a complicated question that she did not understand or did not know the answer to. In those cases, she said, "I do not know, but I will find out and let you know." We took the name and address of the person asking the question, and the campaign staff sent an answer.

After we had done the same type of interview a few times, Rosalynn apologized, "Edna, I'm sorry you have to keep hearing the same things over and over."

Her thoughtfulness touched me. I explained that none of the interviews or speeches sounded the same, even when she went right down the list of questions we had prepared. Rosalynn always considered each question as though it had not been asked before and therefore generally avoided offering canned-sounding answers.

It was hard for Rosalynn to become accustomed to appearing on television I was the only one who knew the uneasiness cameras stirred in her. We never had any hint that the studio personnel or the audiences suspected the butterflies fluttering around inside. As the days passed and cameras became more commonplace to her, she lost most of that uneasiness.

In time, we became our own media experts. No one ever told us about lighting, makeup, or what clothes to wear for television. We learned by experience. As Rosalynn talked on camera, I watched the studio monitor, checking out details. Was her face pale or shiny? I always made sure her hair was in place. I watched for things that might help Rosalynn make a better visual impression. Beyond that, she pulled everything else off by herself.

We quickly learned to make last-minute schedule changes. We always juggled plans in order to appear on an early morning television show, especially early in the week. All that day, and all week long, our vists were more effective because the public was aware that Jimmy Carter's wife was campaigning in their area. Flexibility was a valuable asset. We learned. And we learned fast, because time was short.

As anxious as we were for television coverage, we did turn down several opportunities. One station wanted to film Rosalynn campaigning in a shopping center. She refused. It was not time for that kind of coverage yet. At that point in the political game, we did not want the camera grinding away while she walked up to a stranger and said, "Hello, I'm Mrs. Jimmy Carter, and my husband is running for president." We knew people would not recognize her. Some might laugh, look puzzled, or in all innocence say, "President of what?"

While hometown newspapers do not have the coverage of the large dailies, they are very effective for a fledgling candidate. Since I live in a small town, I know people there pay more attention to their local paper —even if it is only a weekly—than they do the big city publications.

We used one basic plan in contacting the newspapers. Rosalynn introduced herself, then me. She started the handshaking and getting acquainted. Then I suggested an interview.

One persistent problem in the early days involved newspaper receptionists. They always wanted to send us to the society editor or the women's writer. We explained we did not want to be on the society page. We wanted Rosalynn on the front page. If not there, we at least wanted her in the news section. But any page was better than no coverage!

One perceptive editor suggested, "Have your picture made with a local person in each town. Home folks seeing their neighbor's picture look to see who is standing next to him or her."

Jim Gallery, editor of the Palmetto, Florida, paper, suggested a way to multiply the use of our short supply of bumper stickers. He said, "Hold up one of your bumper stickers. They may not take time to read the cutline under the picture, but they'll surely see the Carter bumper sticker—sort of a headline within a headline, or a picture within a picture." We used those ideas often.

Of the dozens of newspaper offices we visited some experiences stand out. One Carter supporter put us in contact with a reporter for a local newspaper. He arranged to meet us at a local restaurant. Evidently he was big league. In a rather dimly lit corner of the main dining room, he waited for us. Around him we saw the paraphernalia of his trade—a personal telephone, the table's "Reserved" sign, and so forth.

He did not eat or suggest that we might be hungry. No one even offered us coffee. He kept talking. I am convinced he was trying to decide if we were two slightly dazed housewives, running around trying to campaign, or if we were serious and dedicated to the nomination of Jimmy Carter. Apparently he decided against us. He did not introduce us to anyone else. As far as we know, he never did print anything about us in his newspaper. He did say, as we left, "If you ever get back into this area again, give me a call."

As I walked out of there, I was disappointed, perhaps even a little angry over his attitude. I thought, *Well, sir, you just don't know what you've missed. Someday you'll be sorry!*

A typical meeting with somewhat skeptical newspaper personnel involved a young woman reporter. She sensed almost immediately the importance of Rosalynn's visit. "Wait a minute," she insisted. "I have to call my editor and check with him." He was not in the office. She called another number. From her conversation, we gathered he was still at home, asleep. Trying to rouse her sleepy boss, she said excitedly, "She's right here. We can really get a good story out of this."

She began jotting down questions he wanted her to ask Rosalynn. Although most of the questions were not new (after awhile, how many new questions can you ask?), the interview was going well.

Then she asked, "How would you restructure Vietnam?"

Rosalynn smiled and answered simply, "I have no idea at all."

Later, reading the interview, we laughed at the fine story she gave Rosalynn, despite her inability to restructure Vietnam.

We received valuable coverage before the primaries began, and people remembered: the newspaper editors and reporters, the television personnel, those at local radio stations. Even small-town disc jockeys remembered that Rosalynn had taken the time to visit them. As they realized the magnitude of a national political campaign, they became impressed that she considered them important enough to come in, visit with them, and ask their help. When the political heat intensified in Florida and the rest of the nation, those small-town leaders did not forget that Rosalynn Carter and "What's her name?" came by one day.

We reached West Panama City Beach, Florida, at lunchtime and stopped at a restaurant for lunch. We placed our order. While waiting for our food, Rosalynn commented on the large number of cars in the parking lot. As we looked around the room, we knew the customers in the restaurant did not begin to account for half the cars.

"Look!" Rosalynn said, pointing. One of the cars bore the sign: PRESS. Looking around inside, I noticed the sign: ROTARY CLUB MEETS HERE, 12:00 NOON, THURSDAYS. It was noon, and it was Thursday. Somewhere, tucked away in a corner of that restaurant, at least one reporter and a roomful of Rotarians were assembled. The hostess pointed out the room. We asked the waitress to hold our order.

My husband is a longtime Rotarian, so I felt quite at home. I went inside, introduced myself to the president of the club, and explained our mission. After he met Rosalynn, he introduced her to the group. She stood behind the portable rostrum and made a brief talk. Rosalynn remembered an admonition Jimmy had given us: "Never go overtime at a noontime club meeting," so she hurried.

She concluded by thanking the president for giving her the time and opportunity to interrupt their meeting. He laughed and said, "Your coming was perfectly timed. Our program had fallen through. I had been wondering what to do!" We could have taken more time!

Pure Carter luck!

After leaving the restaurant, we stopped to phone our headquarters in Atlanta. David Heald, a senior journalism student at the University of Florida in Gainesville, had left a message for us. David, son of Don Elliot Heald, an Atlanta TV executive, had exciting news for us. The Ramada Inn at Ocala was hosting secretaries and their bosses for breakfast the next morning, commemorating National Secretaries Week. People from a wide area around Ocala would be there, and Rosalynn would be introduced at the breakfast. That was exciting news. Just as exciting to us, was the fact that the Ramada Inn innkeeper would put up: WELCOME ROSALYNN CARTER on the motel marquee, if we spent the night there. Her name blazing in lights! What an advertisement, and all free. David was waiting to hear from us, so he could let them know at the Ramada Inn.

"Can you make it?"

"Certainly, we can," Rosalynn said. We had to rush, but we made it. Name recognition was important!

*   *   *   *

The hard work done by hundreds of Carter volunteers finally began paying off by the winter of 1976. Jimmy took the lead in one primary after another. As news of each victory came, the media's attitude changed. Now *they* wanted *us*. We were ready; Rosalynn had learned well, by campaigning through the small towns and out-of-the-way places, to deal with the mess.

From two suitcases in one Chevrolet, we graduated to two cars and a van as we went through New Jersey before the New Jersey, Ohio, and California primaries. Members of the press began to travel with us.

One of the questions frequently asked was, "How can you stand having everybody know everything you do? Even when you sneeze?"

Rosalynn's answer was: "I grew up in Plains, Georgia, population six hundred and eighty-three. Everybody has *always* known everything we did."

The second part of the question brought a chuckle out of us. Rosalynn actually sneezes every morning, when she first gets up. Jack also sneezes, and so does young Jason.

Another frequent question: "Don't you hate all those ugly things the press says about Jimmy?"

The Carters have been in the public eye since the mid-1960s. Whether they are city or state reporters, or on the national level, most of the media people attempt to be fair and accurate. They sometimes misinterpret the facts, but seldom intentionally.

Only twice have I heard either of the Carters say anything harsh to members of the press. The first incident involved a young reporter who came to Plains for an interview with Rosalynn. Although they had never met, she knew of his work, which was often unreliable and often presented distorted facts. Rosalynn asked him, "Why do you need to interview me? You will write what you want to, anyway."

The second time occurred shortly after Andrew Young resigned as ambassador to the United Nations. A reporter, known for his less than factual reporting of the Young incident, made a particularly cutting statement. The president snapped back, "That is not accurate. I wish you would be accurate."

Rosalynn has often spoken of her appreciation for the press. Only recently, she said to another friend in my presence, "I know how important the press is. They can do so much to help the country. They have a responsibility to the people, just as we do. So many good things are happening in this country. Unfortunately, when they cover a worthwhile event, such as a new program in education or mental health, they so often interview someone from a group that disagrees."

* * * *

In those early days of making friends and introducing Jimmy to the people, we had no police escorts, no cadre of press to greet us, and no headlines to announce Rosalynn's presence.

Sometimes friends have asked, "Didn't you get discouraged? Didn't you wonder how one unknown candidate's wife could have any impact or exert any ultimate influence in a national election? Didn't the utter impossibility of the whole enterprise overwhelm you?"

Rosalynn told one person, "I suppose if I had dwelt on the magnitude of it all, I would have felt somewhat overwhelmed. But I also knew we weren't the only ones working. Jimmy was on the trail, working as hard as I was. So were others. I kept thinking each day, *If I can just get to more people and tell them about Jimmy. Let's go to one more newspaper, one more television station, one more radio interview.* The only panic I felt was in not being able to reach enough people with the story. I knew from the beginning that if we could contact enough people, they would elect Jimmy.

"I believe in Americans. I think they are much alike, all over the country. If we can educate them to support a genuinely honest cause, if we can spark their imagination, tell them the straight truth, and involve them, we can do anything. I believed that when we campaigned in 1975 and 1976. I still believe that when we push for any legislation. "I also believe in our approach because it works. It worked in Plains, in Calhoun, in Atlanta, in church groups, and in countless other places. Getting the message across is not always easy. But when it does get across, people respond."

Rosalynn then said firmly, "There are more good, honest, decent people in our country than any other kind. But usually they don't respond until we show them how they can help. Once they know what to do, they will respond."

9

Expectant Grandmothers

THE CAR WAS a black, non-air-conditioned convertible, which is normally fine in the cool Northeast climate, but in May of 1975, New England sweltered in the grip of a rather severe heat wave. However, lack of air-conditioning wasn't the real problem. The car had a malfunctioning water pump! The students who loaned us the car warned us that it suffered from a *slight* mechanical problem. *Slight* really wasn't an apt word! On a regular basis, it had "hot flashes." Of course, when it did, we stopped as soon as possible to get water, asked the service attendants or mechanics to tinker with the car, gave them some brochures, and talked about Jimmy Carter.

What a way for two expectant grandmothers to invade New England, chugging around in a black car with defective innards. But that's what we were doing. We were the advance guard for the Carter Peanut Brigade and, at the same time, we knew that during the summer our daughter Judy was going to give us our first grandchild. We had to prepare for this, too. First of all, how did we get into New England?

When our first two weeks of trial campaigning in Florida were over, we went home to Plains. We had met hundreds and hundreds of people.

For the most part, their names and addresses were written down, but all of these lists had to be made intelligible, so the staff in Atlanta could do the essential follow-up work. So, as we drove home in the dark, we wrote. All the way to Plains and even into the Carter driveway, we tallied names and compiled lists. No car ever had its dome light switched on and off so frequently as that beige Chevrolet.

Rosalynn's first words to Jimmy were: "Jimmy, I can do it. After Florida, I am ready to go anywhere." It was evident that the next "anywhere" had to be New Hampshire. Rosalynn and Jimmy surmised that if they won Florida in the South and New Hampshire in the North, he was in the driver's seat. After we had been home for a few days, she called me and said, "Edna, are you ready to pack? Let's go to New Hampshire."

New Hampshire was brand-new territory for us, but in the next few months we moved in and out of the state so much we came to feel like Northerners from Georgia. On May 25, 1975, nearly a year ahead of the New England primaries, Rosalynn and I arrived in Boston, prepared for our first adventure in New England. Chris Brown, the New England coordinator, met us in Boston, gave us a list of prominent Democrats in the area, then introduced us to the two students whose car we borrowed for a week. To be perfectly frank, I'm convinced that Chris and the other Carter staff people were not sure what to do with us! Rosalynn and I had the feeling they thought we would be a burden to the campaign. You know: "Why are they coming up here? What are they going to do? We don't have time to set up teas!" Soon they found out what two grand-mothers could do!

We got up early, so we could stay ahead of Chris Brown's schedule. However, one important fact had been overlooked in our briefing: Mon-day, May 26, was national Memorial Day. To further complicate mat-ters, New England closed down for the national holiday but actually celebrated on May 29. So, as we moved around Boston that early Mon-day morning, we were confronted with an eerie quiet. We had no idea that big-city Boston would close down so completely!

The Boston Democratic Party headquarters was deserted; not a soul was in sight. With no one to see, we decided to make our own attempt to gain some media coverage. Betty Rainwater, in the Atlanta headquar-ters, had called several times to arrange for Rosalynn to appear on

Boston's WCVB's "Good Morning Show," but had drawn a blank. With nothing to lose, we went to the studio and were admitted by a security guard who asked no questions.

In the semideserted foyer, I used the same technique with the receptionist that we had used in the Florida radio stations. Soon the show's host came out to meet us, embarrassed because he was afraid he had overlooked us on the schedule. We explained our purpose and had a cordial visit, complete with coffee and cookies, while he told us politely that there were no openings on the show that day. However, before we left, he made a small concession: He let Rosalynn do a news spot.

In November, 1979, Rosalynn accepted an invitation to appear as a guest on the same "Good Morning Show." On the way to the studio, she described the first visit's events to Mary Hoyt, her press secretary, who could not believe that we would "ask" to be on the television show. As Rosalynn entered the studio—surrounded by staff, press, and Secret Service—the show's host asked, "Do you remember the time you came and did not get on the program?" Remember? Of course, she remembered! "Well," he said, "you really had us puzzled that day. We could not imagine how you got into the studio. We thought you had an appointment to be on the show and that we had forgotten it."

Rosalynn laughed. "Getting in the gate was no problem. Getting on the show was. Times have changed!"

The one major commitment prearranged for Rosalynn on the 1975 trip was two days away. She was invited to speak at the city of Salem's Bicentennial celebration. Before coming to New Hampshire, we set a goal of visiting all ten counties on our first trip. Logistics prevented it; we did make eight.

As in Florida, we campaigned in those counties with our own brand, our own style of electioneering! We visited radio stations, newspaper offices, television stations, office buildings, and city halls, introduced ourselves, and talked about Jimmy Carter.

After only a few days in New Hampshire, still months away from the primary, we could feel a measure of momentum building for Jimmy. By the time Rosalynn spoke at the Bicentennial celebration in Salem, she had gained a deep feeling for the people of New Hampshire, and a feeling for their roots and history.

On that occasion, Rosalynn laid politics aside for the moment and told the New Englanders of her own roots, deep in south Georgia. To those historically sensitive New Englanders, she described her own history. She told of her mother, Mrs. Allie Smith, the only child of parents whose lineage could be traced back to the beginnings of community life in south Georgia. She told of her mother's growing up in the same house that her grandmother had lived in. She mentioned that she and Jimmy loved that old house and its small farm so much that they bought it, to keep the place in the family. Rosalynn talked about visiting the cemetery in Plains, to look at the tombstones and think about her forebears, who were as important to Georgia as the Salem ancestors had been to New Hampshire.

Then she made her point: "We are so much alike. All across the country, everywhere we go, we meet people with the same dreams and hopes we have. We are all Americans. Our proud history as individuals and as a nation," she told the crowd, "gives strength and reason to everything we do." Speaking conditions were less than ideal, with two large, crowded rooms opening into each other and no public address system, but it didn't matter. The people of Salem heard her words, and I'm positive some of them inwardly embraced this gentle Southern woman.

*   *   *   *

It's remarkable, to me, to see how often a series of simple events occurs that dramatically affects the course of our lives. One blustery March morning in 1975, Vickie Landry was walking up the sidewalk when she met a sandy-haired fellow with a wide grin and no topcoat. She knew he wasn't from New Hampshire! The man said, "Hi. I'm Jimmy Carter, from Georgia. I'm running for President of the United States, and I need your help."

Political candidates abound in New Hampshire, especially as presidential primaries draw near, so Vickie wasn't at all surprised by the man's statement. "But," she remembers, "I felt something from him that made me stop and talk with him for a minute. Before I knew what happened, I filled out a little form on which I requested more information about his campaign."

It was a cold morning, and Jimmy didn't have on a topcoat, so Vickie excused herself and hurried up the street. A few days later, a Carter volunteer called Vickie and asked her, "Can you come to Concord [about eighteen miles north of Manchester] and help us open a Carter for President office?" Though Vickie was pregnant, she immediately agreed to come and do what she could to help.

Her quick visit to the headquarters convinced her the office needed the kind of organizational assistance that Paul, her husband, could give. Thus, before the Landrys knew it, they found themselves up to their eyes in the Carter campaign.

Later, in assessing it all, Paul said, "Jimmy Carter was right on time. We had no place to go. We couldn't stand another McGovern type person, even though the senator has many admirable traits. Senator Muskie didn't even make an attempt, so in the midst of that vacuum, I looked carefully at Carter, and the more I looked, the more I liked what I saw." Jimmy Carter, the maverick, suited the taste of several young, energetic, key New Hampshire Democrats. They were a ready-made match.

Paul and Vickie had an old home in Manchester, which had been in an on-going process of remodeling since they purchased it. The Landrys joined the ranks of Carter Innkeepers, who never knew who or how many would show up for supper or need a bed. Paul and Vickie had the unique distinction of hosting Jimmy Carter and some of his family on the night of the crucial New Hampshire primary.

As we met Paul Landry on our first visit in New Hampshire, Rosalynn understood that he would give us a schedule and escort us on our rounds in Manchester. Paul had received word that Rosalynn and a friend would arrive in Manchester in the late afternoon of May 30, and he was simply to meet them and make them feel welcome and see them on their way. We drove into Manchester on time, according to our timetable, but about four hours early, according to Paul's.

When Rosalynn called to tell Paul that we had arrived, she got a bit of a jolt when Paul said, "Well, where do you go first?"

Paul was equally stunned to hear Rosalynn say, "Wherever you think we should go!"

After a few minutes of panic and embarrassment, Paul and Rosalynn agreed to meet in thirty minutes. It didn't take him very long to introduce us to some good contacts, and these developed into further engagements. That's the way it went, day after day. Of course, all our contacts weren't so smooth. I remember calling an influential labor leader who had been a delegate to the miniconvention in Kansas City.

"Need not waste her time seeing me, lady! I'm waiting for Birch Bayh. Carter's stand on right-to-work laws is no good, if it's like they say!"

To let him know that Rosalynn was interested in him and perhaps to clear up the stand on the right-to-work issue, I persuaded him to give me directions to his house. The dog greeted us with incessant barking. His wife continued to set the table. The man sat in his overstuffed armchair, *never* looking away from the television. Rosalynn presented Jimmy's views on labor as though this were George Meany himself. She might as well have been talking to the wall. He was unconvinced. After a brief amount of time, we commented on the pictures of his children, said our good-byes, and saw ourselves to the door. It takes all kinds of people to make a campaign!

*   *   *   *

During the next months, we hopscotched from one part of the country to another. With the passage of every day, we felt more intensely the pressure of time, because the primaries were getting closer. Also, our first grandchild was on the way! Being new parents is exciting and fun, but being new grandparents is the dividend on the investment. I had planned to take most of August off from the campaign, and Rosalynn had arranged to be as close to Calhoun as her schedule would permit.

On August 6, Judy and Jack had dinner with Beverly and me at our home. At 1:00 A.M., Jack called to say they were leaving for Emory University Hospital in Atlanta. By 7:00 the next morning, August 7, Judy and Dr. Bottomy, who arrived from his Lake Lanier home on his motorcycle, delivered, with Jack's help, eight-pound, eight-ounce, Jason James Carter. The perfect baby—with bright-pink fingernails, just like Jack's, navy blue eyes and strawberry hair, just like Jack's—arrived right on time, just like Jack and all the Carters!

At 7:30 A.M. we heard from Jack, and by 10:30 A.M. we had all talked to one another: grandmothers, grandfathers, great-grandmothers, aunts, and uncles. Soon thereafter, Beverly and I were on our way to meet our newest bundle of joy.

Jimmy didn't miss his chance to announce another special event. For the previous two weeks, he had left his daily schedule with Jack and

Judy. On August 7, he was in Boston, Massachusetts, and was scheduled to be on the "Good Morning Show." When Jack called to tell his father the good news, he was en route to the program. The message was left at the TV station for the new grandfather. Upon receiving the news, Jimmy announced, to the entire watching audience, "Rosalynn and I have a grandson." Appropriately, the television show's host presented him with a large cigar with a blue ribbon tied on it!

The joy of being grandfather and grandmother was to be duplicated for Jimmy and Rosalynn soon after they moved to the White House, when Chip and Caron's son, James Earl III, was born. And on December 19, 1978, Rosalynn and I were co-grandmothers once again, when our granddaughter, Sarah Rosemary, was born. When Jason arrived, Jack and Judy named him after Beverly and Jimmy. When Sarah was born, she was named after Rosalynn and me (My name is Edna Mary.)

Upon being introduced to his grandson, Beverly proudly offered him a miniature gold bulldog. A lifelong cheerleader for the University of Georgia Bulldogs, J. B., as the teenagers had long since dubbed Beverly, wanted to identify Jason as a true Bulldog before his other grandfather, a rival Georgia Tech man, arrived. Jimmy made arrangements to be in Atlanta on that Saturday. When he heard about the bulldog, his quick retort was, "I'm glad Jason has all that gold to hock for his Georgia Tech education!"

Stories of the Tech/Georgia rivalry go on and on.

At less than two years old, Jason was quite aware of it and ready to participate. Coming to dinner at our house one evening, Jason realized that he had on his Georgia Tech T-shirt. To hide it from J. B., he put both little hands over the front of his shirt. No comment from J. B.; he was safe. But when he sat down for dinner, Jason looked down at his hands, still over the gold and white Tech emblem, and asked, "Now how am I going to eat?"

Amy has had her share of the same hassle. When she was small, Beverly gave her a red and black Bulldog rug that she defended fiercely when Jimmy teased he was going to walk on it with his dirty shoes.

The safe arrival of the baby, the pressing needs of the campaign, and the growing sense of Rosalynn's effectiveness in meeting the people, pushed us further afield in 1975. The next four months, through the Christmas season, can be described accurately as hectic, yet exhilarating.

Rosalynn and I, either together or individually, campaigned in several states, traveling by private and commercial planes, until we hit the jackpot: eighteen cities in three days in Oklahoma. It began in Iowa.

10

Grass-Roots Victory

"Do you know what's worse than a grandmother with a new grand-baby? It's two grandmothers with the *same* grandbaby." This friendly aside was made by Verna Oehlert, an Iowa Carter supporter, as we visited her area. Rosalynn and I had to plead guilty to the charge of bragging about our new grandson at every opportunity.

We made our first trip to Iowa in September, 1975. Judy and one-month-old Jason were doing fine, so the two happy grandmothers felt comfortable leaving Georgia to begin traveling again. Now it was Iowa.

The state held a special attraction for me. Though I was reared in Oklahoma, I was born in Davenport, Iowa, so this tour became a personal pilgrimage, as well as a political campaign. I also discovered that my status as a native gave me a bit of leverage while we moved around the state.

Tim Kraft, coordinator for the Midwest, arrived in Iowa only two days ahead of Rosalynn and me, stashed his clothes somewhere, rented a car, and set out to advance the trip.

Our first stop was Des Moines. Once again we had a mini-skirmish about accommodations. Tim had rented two motel rooms for us, one of

which we promptly canceled. We were too busy at first to worry about
the room's rate, but after a second expensive night, we stopped long
enough to say, "Tim, we want to stay with people."

Tim explained that homes with two spare bedrooms were few and far
between, and he wanted us to be comfortable.

"We don't have to have two rooms; we want to be with people, Tim.
Okay?" With that problem settled, we began to stay with friends like
Verna and Howard Oehlert. The Oehlerts live in Clear Lake, Iowa. They
are salt-of-the-earth folks, who support Jimmy 100 percent. Howard, a
former chairman of the Cerro Gordo county commissioners, and his
wife, Verna, are morning-to-night politicos, who delight in working at
the grass-roots level.

The Oehlerts, fortunately for the Carter campaign, became acquainted
with Tim Kraft. As a result, anytime Tim neared their part of the state,
he phoned Verna and cried, "Help!"

Once, needing Verna to make some arrangements for Rosalynn's visit
in the area, he said, "Can you and Howard go with Rosalynn to a
fund-raising event up in O-soggy?"

"Sure," she answered, "but where is O-soggy?" pronouncing the name
the way he had.

"Oh, it's only about thirty miles from here."

"Would you mean *Osage*?" Verna asked. Poor Tim felt the scorch of
that burn for some time.

Howard and Verna hosted a private breakfast for Rosalynn, and then,
almost as though we were moving to a syncopated beat with little wasted
motion, she took us to the newspaper offices and radio and television
studios in surrounding towns and cities. After that occasion, Verna's
comment was, "Rosalynn just fitted in everywhere I took her. She met
everyone easily and impressed all she met."

Some weeks later, the Oehlerts again were working with Tim Kraft,
but this time they were arranging a big event for Jimmy to attend. They
had worked long and hard, lining up people to attend. The reception was
scheduled for 3:00 o'clock in the afternoon. At 1:00 P.M. Tim called from
Des Moines and said, "Verna, I have some bad news. The plane will not
start. We can't come."

"Tim Kraft," Verna shouted, "if you don't get that man up here, after
all the work we've done, I'll kill you!"

Then Tim exploded with laughter, "Now we are even for O-soggy." Jimmy was already on his way.

During the inaugural festivities, Verna met Tim at the White House. By then, he had been named appointments secretary to the president. "Tim," she said, "if I had known how important you were going to be, I never would have made you sleep in the basement during those campaign days."

*   *   *   *

Response in Iowa seemed to be growing. Jimmy Carter was no longer "Jimmy who?" The people-to-people approach made the difference. Time, places, people became a blur, as we passed from one event to another, meeting thousands of new friends.

After a few days in Iowa, Rosalynn and I took a night flight to Chicago. Suddenly we sensed a new awareness, an ability to "feel" the country. We knew the people were responding. We felt a kinship with people, wherever we went.

As we flew to Chicago, Rosalynn, sitting very still, looked through the plane window. Nearing the city, she said, "Look at all those lights down there! Think of all those people—people that we will never know, and yet we'll be responsible for their well-being!" That was a moment of truth for Rosalynn, who, many months before the election, *knew* deep inside that she and Jimmy were going to lead the nation.

As I looked at her while she gazed at the galaxy of lights below, I felt history embracing us. Was she boasting? No! Rosalynn's inner conviction was far too significant for such a cheap emotion. Rather it was as though she was coming to grips with the reality that Jimmy was to be the president and she was to share that responsibility at his side. I did not—could not—comment.

Rosalynn met Jimmy in Chicago and traveled on to Atlanta with him for another campaign engagement, then on to Plains. While Rosalynn went to Plains to see Amy for a few days, I went home to Oklahoma, to meet my parents, Dorotha and Ralph Snyder, who had returned to Ponca City for a visit from their retirement home in Sun City Center, Florida. We had a nice visit together, then, driving their car, I started out to renew acquaintances and arrange future campaign stops for Rosalynn.

In Chickasha, Oklahoma, my friend Sara Ellis, former public-relations director for Oklahoma College for Women, my alma mater, said, "I didn't know about your close relationship with the Carter family, but I had already picked Jimmy Carter out as my candidate. In fact, the other day I called a friend—a dyed-in-the-wool Republican—to tell him that I had found the man who would beat his candidate."

After doing what I could in the time available, my parents and I started back toward Georgia. We stopped in Jackson, Mississippi, to lend help and encouragement to my son, Jim, who had Carter campaign responsibilities in Mississippi, Arkansas, Louisiana, and Alabama, the heart of George Wallace country. Later, in November, Jim escorted Rosalynn and me on a three-day Mississippi campaign trek. We drove the entire length of the state, from Mobile, Alabama, to Memphis, Tennessee, giving our usual emphasis to media coverage and meeting with small groups of key people. One particular comment Rosalynn made on that trip stands out. In fact, it became a maxim for Jim—not only in the campaign, but in his activities since then. She said, "Jim, in order to win people, you must love them. If you don't love them, you cannot win them."

From Mississippi, Rosalynn made a quick trip to Oklahoma, to address a mock convention in Oklahoma City. Madeline MacBean, Rosalynn's personal assistant, wrote Jody Powell a memo concerning the meeting. Madeline explained to Jody that Rosalynn was scheduled to spend all day with small groups of five or six people who are " . . . on the fence, looking for a candidate, and they may grill Rosalynn somewhat intensely on the issues of energy, agriculture, and women's rights. Rosalynn wants to know: Will Jimmy guarantee a woman in his cabinet? Will he balance delegations?" The memo concluded: "Rosalynn has simply said she will do the best she can—whether or not she can specifically answer their questions. But anything you can prepare for her to look over will be helpful."

Constant pressure—from people, interviews, time commitments, lack of sleep, inadequate information—was the order of the day.

*   *   *   *

As we hopped all over the country for Jimmy Carter, fall gave way to winter and Christmastime. Rosalynn and I began to look for gifts for our family between handshaking sessions. If one saw something the other might like, she bought it and made a note in the little, brown expense book. From time to time, we settled accounts. We still do this.

Rosalynn rarely buys large gifts but looks for just the right thing and then makes up her mind in a hurry, when she finds it. The choice is made even easier if the gift can be bought at a bargain! That year she bought electric alarm clocks for some of the family—the kind that beams the time on the ceiling. When she found the clocks on sale, she snapped them up.

All through the fall, we had been in and out of Iowa, but the "brain trusts" felt we should make one more trip before Christmas. Making a cold-weather trip was another matter, for us, however. In September we had experienced an Iowa cold front. It was *cold,* and we were in a very old hotel. We put two pillows at the bottom of the door and towels around the windows, to stop the wind, and we slept in gowns, housecoats, and socks, and used our coats for extra cover. We were two grandmothers from Georgia, campaigning for the presidency, huddled in bed with all our clothes on and the window and door hastily caulked against the cold. It gave us a real lift, as we chuckled at our situation.

Our return to Iowa in real winter was better, because we were prepared. The main purpose of this trip was to attend a Christmas party given by the Democratic Women's Club in Cedar Rapids. Two hundred people attended the formal dinner featuring presidential candidates or their representatives.

Bambi Udall was there on behalf of her father. As Rosalynn stood to speak, she turned to Bambi, saying, "Bambi, you represent your father well. My heart goes out to you because you are here doing this." Tears coming to her eyes, she said, "My children are doing the same thing, scattered across the country somewhere tonight, and I don't even know where they are!" Sitting in the audience, I choked up, appreciating Rosalynn's feelings, and wondered where *my* children were. It was a touching occasion.

Christmas was upon us, and we were anxious to get home to our families, but we had a few more assignments. Rosalynn did radio, television, and newspaper interviews. The last event of the trip called for us to meet a shift change at a factory. In freezing weather, we arrived on schedule—very early in the morning, before daylight—with our brochures and Carter posters on sticks. The workers avoided us like the plague. In the dark, the employees saw us carrying signs and thought we were pickets! Hastily the posters disappeared into the trunk of the car, and we were better received. Then it was home to Georgia for Christmas.

Jack, Judy, and Jason spent part of the Christmas holidays in Calhoun with Beverly and me, but Santa Claus made his first visit to young Jason Carter via the chimney at the Carter home in Plains.

The Christmas season was short for us. As soon as possible, Jack, Judy, Lucie, and I went to spend all of January, 1976, in Florida, getting ready for that critical primary. A month in Florida was a long time. Judy wanted five-month-old Jason near, so Lucie, my younger daughter, agreed to take care of him, and Jason became the youngest member of the campaign team. Often when Jack and Judy were on the campaign trail, Kate Langford, Beverly's mother, kept Jason. After each additional trip, however, Judy grew increasingly reluctant to be separated from him for such long periods of time. She very candidly admitted, "If I were away from Jason, campaigning, I felt guilty because I had left him. When I was at home with him, I felt guilty because Mother, Jack, Rosalynn, and Jimmy and all the others were out working so hard that I could not let them down."

We had been in Florida only a few days when Hamilton Jordan panicked and sent Jack and Judy to Iowa. In fact, he sent *all* the Carters back to Iowa, and I was to go back to Oklahoma (the Oklahoma caucuses followed Iowa's) before we invaded New Hampshire again. These dramatic changes in plans were disrupting to everyone. Just as I began to be concerned about Lucie's staying with Jason alone in such a new place, Rosalynn called, worried about her mother, Miss Allie. Post office regulations forced Miss Allie to retire on January first, and she was very unhappy. We found the perfect solution to two problems: Mother Allie would come to help Lucie with Jason. She came to Florida the day Jack and Judy left.

I had brought my winter clothes to Florida, because I expected to go from there to Oklahoma and then on to New Hampshire. When Hamilton sent his distress call, Judy, who had not packed for cold weather, took my winter clothes and headed immediately to Iowa. Taking inventory of what was left, I found the only coat I had with me was a light raincoat. When I got off the plane in Oklahoma City, David Hales, our campaign coordinator, said, "Is that the only coat you have? It gets cold and windy here in January!"

To which I replied, "Yes, this is the only coat I have, and if you are any kind of coordinator, you will get me a better one, or better weather." Believe it or not, the cold air and blustery winds moved out, and for those three days, the weather was spring beautiful. The temperature was above fifty degrees, with almost no wind at all. Jimmy did have gifted people working for him!

I was provided a somewhat fatigued Cadillac to travel in Oklahoma, while making arrangements for what turned out to be one of the most remarkable jaunts in the entire campaign.

En route from Ponca City to Oklahoma City the evening of the Iowa caucuses, I turned on the car radio and heard the newscaster saying: "Jack Carter, son of candidate Jimmy Carter, ran a red light and had an automobile accident." They gave no more details. The news was a little frightening. Worried, I went on to Oklahoma City, one hundred miles south.

My borrowed car had run very well the past two days, but the left window would not come back up, and there were no instrument lights for night driving. As it got darker and I heard no more news, I hurried a little faster on the almost deserted interstate highway. Thirty miles from Oklahoma City, in a fifty-five-mile-an-hour zone, I met a state trooper. Nothing would satisfy him but to take my license, so he did!

Creeping into the Oklahoma City headquarters with my ticket, I hurriedly put a call through to Jack, in Des Moines. With a great sigh of relief, I learned that he did have an accident, but no one was hurt. "What were you doing?" I asked.

"Looking at the frozen river!" he exclaimed.

I had never seen a frozen river, either!

The trooper had taken my license and told me that I had to pay forty-five dollars to get it back. I didn't have forty-five dollars with me. Without the license, I would have a very difficult time traveling. The next morning, in grand-old campaign style, the young people in the headquarters emptied their pockets, pooled enough money, and drove to Guthrie to bail out my driver's license.

Then the news came: victory in Iowa. Victory—victory! It was just what we needed.

The news flashed across the country and into the capitals of the world: "Jimmy Carter wins the 1976 Iowa caucus!" It also zoomed into the villages, hamlets, towns, and cities where the Peanut Brigade, a group of volunteers traveling for Jimmy Carter, had been campaigning during the past months. It was a celebration. The Iowa caucuses had never seemed this important, before. It gave us recognition, credibility, and a boost of incalculable value in the eyes of the questioning. To our supporters everywhere, it gave a thrust big enough to challenge them to greater efforts.

After the Iowa triumph, when Rosalynn landed in Oklahoma City for our major Oklahoma effort, she was met for the first time by a crowd of reporters. Though the press corps was not ready to travel with her, they took dozens of pictures and filed their stories from the airport.

David Hales, our coordinator, had arranged a schedule of marathon proportions for this Oklahoma push: We were to shake hands, sip coffee, eat snacks, and talk about Jimmy Carter in *eighteen* towns and cities in three days! And we did it.

*   *   *   *

Several months after Jimmy Carter was elected president, I was visiting at the White House. Rosalynn asked, "Why don't you go downstairs, to the reception in the State Dining Room, and have lunch with the people from Iowa who are here for the domestic policy briefing? I'll be down later. Floyd Gillotti, Lorna Kunath, Joan and Jim Reynolds, Hazel and Charles Hammer, Phyllis Hughes, Henry Cutler, and other friends will be there." I hurried downstairs.

As I walked into the beautiful room, I spotted Floyd and several of our other friends. We gathered around and talked Iowa politics. In the midst of the conversation, Jim Reynolds, there with his wife, Joan, made an interesting comment. He said, "You know, Rosalynn's got the ability to see people for *real.* I imagine that most of the people in this room have had a conversation with her—a conversation, many times, in the middle of a crowd, where she looked at and listened to just them. That's not typical of people in politics. She owns her own horsepower." I am not exactly sure what he meant by that last statement, but it impressed me as a compliment. We all laughed!

Henry Cutler, from Waterloo, spotted me and came over to chat.

"Hey, I'm getting to be an old hand at coming to the White House. In fact, as I looked around the group, I do believe that everyone has been here before. The other day I was with some of my longtime Republican friends at the country club, bragging about getting ready to come to the White House. They were really a little envious. Most of them have supported successful Republican candidates and have never been invited to the White House."

Later that evening, when I mentioned Henry's conversation to Rosalynn, she said, "Of course. Jimmy and I agreed that when we got to the White House, we would open it to the American people for as many events as possible. We do not want the people to feel isolated from the government. This house belongs to the American people. They should enjoy it."

She kept her word. The beautiful rooms on the state floor and the smaller ones on the ground floor echo the sounds of every imaginable event. Groups who volunteer for programs and projects meet Rosalynn and Jimmy for planning and reporting sessions. Leaders in mental-health programs, refugee relief, family concerns, business and industrial development, religious and benevolent ventures gather with the First Family to receive input and encouragement.

An important thrust of the Carter White House has been briefings on matters of vital importance, to which community leaders from every walk of life are invited. In the East Room, the president and his top advisers talk about national problems and answer questions. In the State Dining Room, these same leaders congregate for receptions, where important relationships and understandings develop. The White House staff, ushers, and other assistants give devoted service to the First Family and to the American people in the Carters' open White House. And, really, the significant key to it all was when Iowa went for Jimmy Carter.

11

Change of Pace

ROSALYNN and I, morning newspapers in hand, were finishing breakfast in the family dining room in the White House. There is seldom an informal Carter meal without someone's bringing something to the table to read.

This particular morning, as we read and talked about the news, Rosalynn suddenly stopped the conversation and swiftly picked up the phone by the dining-room table and asked the operator to find David Rubenstein. She said to me, "Before I leave for my trip, I have to check on *this,* " pointing to an article in the paper. It was typical. There is seldom a totally private moment, when you live in the White House. Pressures of all kinds, domestic and foreign, personal and public, demand attention. Because of these invaders, Rosalynn has to find a way to get away for a change of pace.

Prior to 1970 and Jimmy's term as governor, Plains was the place to get away *from.* From 1970 through 1976, Plains was the place to get back *to.*

When the boys were growing up, the Carters, like many American families, took vacations providing a change of pace and educational experiences.

The summer after Jack graduated from high school, they took an educational trip. After three weeks of touring rural Mexico, they were easing across an especially bumpy railroad crossing one mile from the Mexican border, when their car slammed to a halt with a loud noise. By some strange quirk, one side of the front bumper had become dislodged and had jammed down between the cross ties in the track. Try as they would, it would not budge! They pulled together, then tried jacking up the car. No luck. They had no idea of the train schedule, and all the family had visions of a Mexican locomotive bearing down on the car. Good bye auto! Finally, when all else failed, they had to call a wrecker and pay $100 to get off the railroad track. The only consolation at having to pay the $100 was that they didn't have to buy a new car!

Long before it was the rage, the Carters enjoyed family camping. In 1963, Jimmy, with his bent for adventure, encouraged by his three energetic, excited young sons, persuaded Rosalynn to take a camping trip up the East Coast to Washington, D.C. The entire family, Rosalynn included, loved it—well, most of it.

After a night or two on the trail, the Carter clan worked out a plan for setting up camp so that, in a matter of minutes, the big umbrella tent was up, the cook stove and utensils were ready for use, and the boys were off exploring the area. Rosalynn loved the freedom of camping. She did not have to worry about schedules, clothes, or makeup. It was a good time to be with one another, to let the boys roam through the woods, and to have time for oneself in the peace and serenity of nature.

With no television and little outdoor light, bedtime came early. Besides, Jimmy got them up at daybreak, to get an early start. Five people in a large tent, sleeping on air mattresses, is not too bad, unless three of them are wiggly, giggly, whispering, punching young boys.

As they entered the Great Smoky Mountains, signs began to appear: BEWARE OF THE BEARS ! "Bears? Great! Where?" It was another story, when they *really* came. That night, Smoky the Bear stole the bacon, gutted the cooler, and ransacked the garbage can—all right outside their tent, which suddenly seemed quite thin and fragile.

At one point, it rained and rained—buckets of rain. Late one afternoon, after they had stopped and set up camp, Jimmy and the boys drove the car into a shallow creek, to wash some of the grime away. While they splashed in the stream, Rosalynn cooked their supper, a favorite dish of ground beef and canned spaghetti. When it was done, she set the hot pan on one end of a rickety, split-log bench. Without thinking, she sat down on the other end, flipped the bench, and dumped the supper on the ground. That was the last straw: the rain, the last package of ground beef, the ruined spaghetti, and no supper! She wept.

When Jimmy and the boys heard her crying, they ran to see what happened. After a little comforting, the problem was solved by a search through the food supplies. Jimmy found a box of pancake mix and in no time whipped up a big batch of hotcakes.

Days on the camping trail, with mainly cold showers in rather primitive campgrounds, convinced Rosalynn it was time for better accommodations for a night or two. In Washington, she persuaded Jimmy to stop at a motel and check on the availability of rooms. "Eighteen dollars a night? Too much," Jimmy declared. But after the manager came down two dollars, Rosalynn got her bath and bed.

From time to time during the years, Rosalynn and Jimmy have gone to the Georgia coast—either to Sea Island, Sapelo Island, or Cumberland Island—for vacations. Of particular significance was the sweet week at Sea Island after the 1976 November general election. Two years of incredible work had paid off. The entire family savored their victory during those days of fishing, tennis, jogging, and gearing up for the presidency.

                    *   *   *   *

Going back home to Plains took on a different significance after the Carters moved to the governor's mansion. Remember going home, back to the town where you grew up, back to the place filled with family ties and memories? I had that feeling when we went back to Iowa and Oklahoma. Rosalynn felt that when she went back to Plains. She and her family knew every road and trail in Plains and Sumter County. Nearly everyone in town was a friend or relative. The town felt proud of Governor Carter, so it was a pleasant time of affirmation for the Carters, when they returned to Plains for a weekend visit.

Many have overheard Rosalynn say, "I love my house in Plains. I love my things there. It's my haven. The people in Plains are my friends. I am always so glad to go home to Georgia." Between the closing of Jimmy's administration as governor and the campaign of 1975, Rosalynn redecorated their four-bedroom, one-story house in Plains. Little had been done to the house, beyond routine maintenance, since its construction in 1960. Rosalynn, who likes to decorate and is good at it, found going to Plains to work on the house gave her time and space to think, even though she had to squeeze the time between official duties. The necessity proved to be fun and a therapeutic diversion.

She painted each room herself, including the ceilings in the living room and the dining room. Later she taught me how to paint, when we helped Jack and Judy with that unforgettable move in Athens. Hard work had never been a fear of mine, but I confess that cleaning and painting *that* house was not a pleasant diversion or a good change of pace.

In the dining room in the house in Plains, there is a small but elegant crystal chandelier that Rosalynn loves. When they bought it in the 1960s, she was so proud of it. After they came home from the governor's mansion, Rosalynn walked into the dining room and looked at the chandelier with that, "it may not be as big or as elegant, but it's mine" look. No doubt she will have more of those same feelings after leaving the White House. What is so special about Plains to Rosalynn? What's so special about going home to Plains? The people are important, of course. But to understand Rosalynn's feelings, one has to realize she has a real love affair with the Carter home, where they have lived for so many years.

The family room—with its beamed, vaulted ceiling—is the heart of the home. On occasions when the family is together, they congregate here. The big wood-burning fireplace is surrounded by inviting chairs and a comfortable sofa. Large, gold area rugs, with heavy knotted fringe, center each sitting area. All wall space at one end of the large room is covered with shelves of books. A side wall displays pictures and memorabilia from many high points in their political and family life. Displayed prominently in this room, too, are several original paintings, selected as the beginning of a still-pursued interest in art.

At the right of the fireplace is the door into the breakfast room and well-arranged kitchen. I asked Judy what she thinks about when musing over family times here. She said, "I picture the kitchen, with a large platter of sandwiches and a big bowl of soup on the counter and everyone walking by to help themselves before sitting in the breakfast area to chat."

Annette says she remembers prepresidential gathering days as times when Rosalynn would say, "You visit with each other. This is my kitchen. When I come to your house, I'll talk while you cook. One of the things I liked most about visiting my mother-in-law was that she did the cooking and washed the dishes. And I want to do the same for you."

Rosalynn loves to cook; it is a diversion for her. When the family was growing up, she always did her own cooking, although she admits Jimmy taught her how. "Where he learned to cook," she says, "I don't know. He probably got hungry." During the transition period between the Ford presidency and Jimmy's assuming office, he and Fritz Mondale, as president and vice-president elect, held their private planning sessions in Plains, cooking their own meals while Rosalynn and I attended the Mexican president's inauguration. Rumors are that Mondale is a good cook, too! Rosalynn has her chance to cook in the White House on Saturdays and Sundays. On these evenings, she has requested that none of their chefs be there.

Remodeling of the Plains house brought the screened-in porch into the family room as a sunny solarium with large, glass sliding doors. Potted plants, in Jack's handmade macrame hangers, decorate the airy room. A rustic pine chaise lounge, built by Jimmy early in their marriage, is one of the most frequently used pieces of furniture in the house. When the remodeling was completed, the original carport had been paneled, to serve as a spacious, warm, library-office for Jimmy. This is Rosalynn's favorite room!

During the campaign years, after the Carters moved back home, Plains represented a *breathing* place, not a *resting* place. Life moved too rapidly during those months for there to be much rest for anyone. But it was always good for the Carters to be home—to be able to unwind.

Since moving to the White House, Jimmy and Rosalynn find returning to Plains is far more complicated; as a result, their visits have become less frequent. When the president travels, elaborate communication and security systems go with him. Weekends in Plains, Calhoun, or anywhere other than established retreats, pose involved and expensive arrangements, so the Carters usually stay at the White House or go to Camp David.

Since the days of Franklin Roosevelt, Camp David, tucked away in Maryland's Catoctin Mountains, has been used by presidents as a place to get away, to rest, and to think.

Rosalynn and Jimmy went to Camp David for the first time in late February, 1977. After exploring the retreat, Rosalynn said, "Why have we waited so long to come?"

After visiting Camp David, I can readily understand why Jimmy and Rosalynn and other First Families thoroughly appreciate the retreat. The accommodations are not luxurious, but they are extraordinarily comfortable. With pool, sauna, tennis, bowling, and gorgeous walking and hiking trails, Camp David is the perfect place for a president and his family to rest, while still being able to effect instantaneous contact with the country and the world. Camp David is not a place for Jimmy and Rosalynn to forget pressures, but at least he can get daily briefings and hold discussions in a quieter setting, and the feeling of pressure is lessened somewhat.

Rosalynn always takes a briefcase full of work to Camp David, but I know that sometimes it's unopened when she returns to the White House. Camp David, for Rosalynn, often provides the scene and circumstance for a clearer focus on life.

One time she said, "For me, Camp David is a good place to get away from pressures, from the clamor of the Washington press corps, and just to be alone with my family. I have a chance to think about what I'm doing and about this country, to focus on God, and generally to enjoy the beauty and peace of the mountains."

In the mountains, Rosalynn relaxes with easy reading, rides bicycles, hikes or jogs, and in good weather, swims.

Rosalynn and Jimmy frequently invite friends to Camp David. One weekend, at just the right time for us, Jimmy called Beverly and said, "Come on up to the mountains. I want to know what is going on in Georgia."

Beverly, who really prefers *not* to get out of Gordon County, nonetheless accepted the invitation. His favorite expression is "I'd rather have a flat tire in Fairmount, Georgia, than go to Washington." Perhaps some readers who have lived in a small, rural community all their lives can understand Beverly's feeling.

Anyway, on that occasion we caught an early bird flight to Washington and drove from the airport to the retreat in Maryland. We walked the trails, talked family and politics, and enjoyed a reunion with good friends.

During the afternoon, Rosalynn and I decided to ride bicycles. I had never ridden a ten-speed bicycle and was not particularly anxious to learn how on mountain trails. Rosalynn kept encouraging and coaxing, "Come on, Edna. . . . Of course you can. . . . Sure you can." And so I did. I found that riding through the wooded area of Camp David is therapy for the soul. One never knows when a deer will come to the edge of the forest and look out over the surrounding pasture. The trails are well planned and maintained. Hardwoods and evergreens abound, with mountain laurel, red raspberries, and wild honeysuckle growing as a ground cover. It is beautiful. I can understand why Franklin Roosevelt first named the place Shangri-la.

A change of pace for Rosalynn may involve tennis, jogging, fishing, or any number of things. In Georgia, Rosalynn sometimes brought Amy to Calhoun, donned her jeans, and fished for hours at our pond. Those were worm-fishing days. Now she can fish with a fly rod.

She's tried her hand at various sports. In high school she played basketball on the girls' varsity team, and in recent years she has taken up tennis. It was not a big game in Plains a number of years ago, because the town had no public courts. But for almost a year at the White House, Jimmy played with her nearly every day, pushing her to succeed. Now, she's good at it. In fact, she's become quite single-minded about playing tennis proficiently.

This single-mindedness toward tennis is characteristic of Rosalynn. Being single-minded is not a fault, but it can be a handicap. When the boys were young, Rosalynn wanted to learn to play golf. Have you ever tried hitting the little white ball with, "Mom, he's pushing me!" or "How much longer?" or "I want a drink of water," disturbing your concentration? Three little boys caused too much confusion on the golf course. So, rather than leave them at home, she left them at the movies in Dawson, Georgia, and let them sit through several runs of the feature while she struggled with her game. When she injured her hand in the door of the safe at the warehouse and could not play for a while, Rosalynn began to evaluate the situation. She felt she was spending too much time playing golf—and her boys were spending too much time watching "B" movies! Decision time; the end of golf for her.

*   *   *   *

Since Rosalynn cannot retreat to Camp David all the time, what does she do to get away from pressures while at home? She sews, reads, plays the piano, arranges flowers, and spends time with Amy.

Home is the second floor of the White House. The center hall, extending the entire east-west length of the mansion, is decorated and arranged like a long, elegant living room. Graceful period furniture for sitting and lounging, a television set, stereo, and video-tape set invite Rosalynn, Jimmy, and Amy and Amy's frequent guests to congregate, watch television, snack out of the family kitchen, and do what you would do in your your home. In spite of the ostentation of the six large crystal chandeliers, the Oriental rugs, and other such furniture, it is homey, friendly, and comfortable.

The third floor of the White House contains several guest rooms for the many personal and family friends who visit. The boys and their friends make regular use of the billiard and ping-pong room, which Rosalynn decorated with pictures, many of which have been cover selections for magazines. Of course, special pictures of grandchildren and family are scattered throughout.

Probably the most delightful room in the family part of the house is the octagonal solarium on the third floor. Rosalynn made this many-windowed room sparkle with yellows, blues, and greens. It serves as a place for much informal entertaining, and the grandchildren especially love the area. Access to the solarium is by way of a rather steep ramp. One of our favorite sights is Jason, in his fuzzy Superman pajamas, sliding on his backside down the hardwood floor at the edge of the ramp's carpet. The solarium overlooks the south lawn, with a breathtaking view of the Jefferson Memorial, past the Washington Monument.

Jimmy, a movie fan, frequently retreats into a good film. He makes regular use of the small, comfortably appointed family theater on the ground level of the East Wing, often inviting friends and staff to watch with him. Rosalynn, though she does not dislike movies, doesn't share his enthusiasm for the cinema. But Jimmy and Amy usually persuade her to join them. Jimmy gets up at 5:30 A.M. and goes to his office, but Rosalynn doesn't like to get up that early. By dinnertime, Jimmy is ready to relax, watch a movie, and go to bed; whereas Rosalynn, who starts her day later, needs to work late.

Sewing is a diversion for Rosalynn. In her dressing room there is a rack lined with dresses, skirts, blouses, and suits needing alterations. In a corner of the room, she has a sewing machine. She loves to snatch sewing time and attacks the alterations with enthusiasm. Recently she bought a suit on sale, that was too long at the shoulders. She took the sleeves off the jacket, shortened the shoulders, and put it all back together, creating a smart-looking outfit that fits just right.

Also, Rosalynn loves gardening. Her backyard in Plains is filled with tall, longleaf pine trees, azaleas, camellias, daffodils, and other native south Georgia plants. She planted most of the flowers and shrubs herself.

In the governor's mansion, Rosalynn's landscaping abilities were well used. She helped plan and supervised the landscaping of the grounds of the two-year-old structure. To fund the project, she planned and published a book about the mansion and its priceless federal-period antiques.

To keep her gardening touch while she was in Atlanta, she created a small garden in the backyard of the governor's mansion and tended it herself. A friend gave her 120 rose bushes that she had planted. One of her pastimes at the mansion was to dress in old jeans, shirt, and floppy hat and work in the garden among the roses. She laughed when tourists came and went without recognizing the gardener.

Reading is another escape for Rosalynn. Growing weary of heavy reports, she enjoys light reading such as novels, mysteries, and other books from the best-seller list, but hesitates to discuss her literary fare. On occasion she turns the jacket of the book wrong side out to protect her reading privacy.

Both for relaxation and spiritual strengthening, Rosalynn and Jimmy read the Bible every night. For the past several years, they have read together from the Spanish Bible.

Several months after moving to Washington, Rosalynn called me, saying, "I have not been home in so long, I miss my friends. Next week I have to be in Georgia and will have some time. Can you get some of our friends together for lunch?"

I called our cooking-school instructor, Ursula Kneusal, for suggestions, and she immediately said, "Come to my house. I will fix something
fun." Betty Gail Gunter added to the festivities by bringing us 1977
Christmas keepsakes—little wooden mice! Rosalynn brought us the stories of what she had been doing in Washington, the endless schedules,
happenings, and events. Mixed with her fascinating anecdotes about her
new life were our warm and funny "remember whens." Her endless
delight with both worlds underscored what we all knew to be true—she
would always be the same person she was before she left Plains.

All in all, however, Amy is Rosalynn's best change of pace. Amy Lynn
Carter, born October 19, 1967, has been a great source of joy to the
Carters. When Rosalynn told Jimmy she was pregnant, he immediately
announced to a crowd of 700 at a Swainsboro, Georgia, church that his
long-awaited daughter was on the way. Many of us during those days
of waiting wondered if he would have to eat his words, but he didn't
worry. He was convinced it would be a daughter.

The strength of their love for Amy has undergirded her in her very
public life. They have attempted to keep her from the prying eyes of the
press and the idly curious public. When Rosalynn and Jimmy were
campaigning, Amy was well cared for by her grandmothers, uncles,
aunts, older cousins, and a townful of good friends. Miss Lillian—
"Grandmomma" to her grandchildren and Amy's official babysitter—
stated flatly that one and all could go to Washington, if they left Amy
in Plains! She missed her very much, and still does!

Even though she has spent her life in a public fishbowl, Amy seems
to be a well-adjusted young lady who has taken her fame and publicity
in stride. Rosalynn and Jimmy insist that she is allowed to be herself.

Rosalynn has sometimes felt guilty about having to leave Amy because
of the responsibilities of her role, but I've heard her say, "Actually, I
spend more time with Amy than I did with the boys. I schedule time with
her, and nothing interferes. I was with the boys more of the time, but
our attention was on other things, rather than on them. The time with
Amy is just for the two of us."

Part of their time together is spent in sharing violin lessons. For
Rosalynn, one of the most pleasant events in the week is the ride to and
from the lessons. Music has always been a pleasant interlude for Rosalynn, who plays the piano for her own enjoyment. Amy has a talent for

music, and though the newspapers make much of the fact that she doesn't enjoy practicing, she is diligent in her learning and certainly no greater problem than any other youngster who goes through the trials of mastering an instrument.

Amy is creative. Last year, at a yard sale, she bought some stuffed animals for five cents each. She took them apart and, with imagination, created her own new stuffed animals out of the old parts.

A beautiful curio cabinet in Rosalynn's White House bedroom symbolizes the special relationship between mother and daughter. Perhaps in earlier years former First Ladies used this antique cabinet to protect precious bric-a-brac from far-flung places. Today it holds priceless objects made unique not because of their age or artistry but because they came from Amy, as gifts from a growing daughter to her mother: a baby-food jar, containing a dried arrangement with tiny pinecones on top; a piece of pottery from a trip Amy made; a doll in a dress identical to the one Amy wore to the inaugural ball; a special paperweight—an oyster and tiny pearl.

One night shortly after the inauguration, we were gathered in the family quarters of the White House, watching television and talking. Amy wandered into Jimmy's and Rosalynn's room, crawled up on their big, four-poster canopied bed, and fell asleep. After a while, Rosalynn asked Jimmy to take Amy to her own bed. I paid little attention to that quick family exchange, until Jimmy came out of the bedroom with Amy in his arms. He turned up the center hall, Amy's long hair hanging over his arm, and with the inimitable Carter gait, carried his sleeping daughter toward her room. For an instant, father and daughter were framed against the fan window at the far end of the hall. My mind snapped the picture, which entered my own archive of memories. I was grateful Amy had a mother with sufficient sensitivity to know the value of a dried arrangement in a baby-food jar and a father with arms big enough not only to embrace a nation, but to carry his nine-year-old daughter to her bed.

12

Front-Runners

"HELLO, RED two. This is the control tower. We have lost contact with you. Hello Red two. Hello Red two. This is airport control. I don't know where you are. Repeat: We have lost contact with you. You are out of our range!"

We had been in the air for a good while when we heard the control tower squawk the urgent message. I looked out of the small window and noted quickly the proximity of a green hill. I shut my eyes. We were lost in a private plane; there was nothing I could do about it. Later, Rosalynn remarked, "How could you go to sleep at a time like that?" I pointed out to her that there was a difference between closing one's eyes and going to asleep. Panic was not the solution, at that moment. I didn't know where we were, either! So I rested my eyes. Rosalynn didn't seem to be assured by my logic.

That situation was typical of the campaign from the beginning of January, 1976, until the Democratic convention. I look back at those days remembering them as a constant blur of activity, noise, snacks, hellos and good-byes, and all the other typical facets of the American electoral process.

*   *   *   *

Up since 4:30 A.M. , waiting in the dark lobby at 5:30, it was obvious
to Rosalynn and me that Charlie Walker, Rosalynn's campaign advance
man, had overslept. Everyone was ragged and tired—most of all,
Charlie. When he did not show, our call jarred him awake. Chagrined,
he told us where our first factory stop was. We grabbed our materials
and a cab and raced to meet the early shift. In our best campaign style,
we began to hand out brochures. The first worker pointedly threw our
materials on the ground. Looking Rosalynn in the face, he said, "Lady,
we make B-1 bombers!" The factory was down to 10 percent employ-
ment. Jimmy had come out against the B-1 bomber that week. An office
worker took us through the offices, then we hastily retreated, to regroup
with a red-faced Charlie Walker.

That's the way it was: attack, retreat, win some, lose some. All the time
praying, working, hoping for another victory, another primary success.
Our schedule became our master. Our lives were dictated by the advance
person. Our families—all of them involved one way or another in the
campaign—became voices at the other end of a phone call that inevitably
seemed to end with, "Bye for now; I've got to rush to make an appointment."

For example, although Jeff and Annette Carter traveled to various
parts of the country, they concentrated their efforts in New England.
They were newlyweds (married April 6, 1975), and for some strange
reason, they insisted on working together! For the final New Hampshire
drive, they rented an apartment in Manchester at what seemed a good
price. But they had not reckoned with the bitter cold of a New England
winter. Annette says, "Our apartment was adequate, but we were cold
all the time. On one of the coldest nights, the wind whipped around and
the cold penetrated the windowpanes, almost as if they were not there.
We were desperate, so Jeff poured water around the windows; the water
quickly froze, providing insulation against the cold wind. Not bad, for
a south Georgia boy! The idea worked, but we were still cold!"

Because Jeff and Annette had no children or any other family encum-
brances, their campaign leaders wanted to use them full-time. As a result,
they campaigned seven days a week, for many weeks at a time. Annette
said, "Sometimes we pleaded for a free Sunday, but our requests were
seldom granted." After leaving New Hampshire, Jeff and Annette cam-

paigned in thirty-nine other states, going to some states several times. For all of us, the demands of abnormal hours, the unusual exposure to the public, the constant pressure of dealing with criticism, and so forth, stretched our personal resources to the limit. Annette, who was young and looked even younger, was inexperienced and sensitive to rude, sharp comments. Several occasions at the beginning of the campaign caused her grief and tears. But it did not take long for her to harden to these situations. I've heard her say since then, "Campaigning is great—when it is over!"

Communication lines hummed in every direction. Plans were coordinated, as well as could be expected, under the hectic circumstances. Jimmy's climbing popularity brought about a definite change in scheduling for the entire family. Newspapers, television, and magazines asked for interviews. A news release of January 15, 1976, reveals Rosalynn's new status:

> Rosalynn Carter, wife of presidential candidate Jimmy Carter, will hold a news conference Tuesday, January 20, 1976, from 7:55 to 8:25 a.m. in the Press Room adjacent to Gate 11 in the Braniff terminal at Dallas/Fort Worth Airport.
>
> The news conference will be the first public appearance of any member of the Carter family following the initial vote in the Iowa delegate selection process on January 19. Carter, former chief executive of the state of Georgia, is expected to do well in the Iowa precinct caucuses and will be one of only a few major candidates for the presidency who will make the attempt to qualify in all 31 senatorial districts in Texas for the May 1st primary.
>
> After the news conference, Mrs. Carter will fly from Dallas/Fort Worth Airport to Oklahoma, where the state's delegate selection will take place February 7.

People love a winner.

By late January, letters began to arrive, inviting Rosalynn and Jimmy to all kinds of events. One was from Mrs. Alice Mason of New York City, who hosted a Sunday-morning brunch for Rosalynn. She had arranged a $250-a-plate dinner for Jimmy and thought she could charge $150 per person for Rosalynn. I'm not at all sure that the lower price for Rosalynn's presence was a true indication of her value in the campaign! (A woman's point of view, of course.) What a drastic change from a few months ago, when it was "Jimmy who?" and "Rosalynn who?" This was a new day; we had come from scrambling for attention to deciding which invitation to accept!

Rosalynn began 1976 by addressing a Woman of the Year banquet sponsored by Myers Publishing Company. The banquet signaled another first for Rosalynn: Mary King, from Washington, would help with the speech, if she wanted her to. Abundant invitations and a speech writer —times were changing!

Rosalynn prefers writing her own speeches, but throughout the years in the White House, others have helped her with the research for various events. Nowadays, Mary Hoyt, who has been press secretary to Rosalynn since 1976, often does preliminary work on the speeches, collecting information and organizing outside research. Also, when Rosalynn asks, the presidential speech writers provide "talking points." More often than not, she writes and edits her own material.

February, 1976, included a "Good Morning, America" interview. A memo came to Rosalynn, saying that an ABC limousine would come to take her to the show. After the interview with David Hartman, the limousine took her to LaGuardia Airport, to leave for Boston. On and on it went: receptions . . . interviews. . . . Look at Rosalynn's schedule over a twenty-six-day period:

January	5	Iowa/Dubuque
	6	Iowa
	7	Iowa
	8	Iowa/Atlanta
	9	Florida/Orlando
	10	Florida
	14	Plains/Mississippi
	15	Mississippi
	16	Mississippi
	17	Mississippi/Plains
	18	Plains
	20	Oklahoma

21	Oklahoma
22	Oklahoma/Florida
23	Florida
24	Florida/Atlanta
25	New York/Plains
29	New England
30	New England
31	New England

In our judgment, none of these invitations, important as they were, could take the place of the people-to-people campaign, so Rosalynn and I continued trekking together.

*   *   *   *

On a cold, snowy day in early February, 1976, we arrived back in New England. This time Ken Curtis, former governor of Maine, met us, accompanied by a CBS television crew that filmed every detail of Rosalynn's deplaning. As we gingerly tiptoed across the ice near the plane, Jim Jackson, of the campaign staff, stuck his head out the terminal door and shouted, "I can tell you're from Georgia!" All we needed was a broken ankle or two!

By now, some of the media were identifying Jimmy as the front-runner. This spurred us on. We increased our efforts. We continued to follow the same kind of schedule as we had in other places—radio stations, nursing homes, factory-shift changes, and any other place where we could meet all kinds of people. In one mall, Rosalynn routinely said to a man with a crew cut, "I am Mrs. Jimmy Carter, and I want you to vote for my husband."

"No!" the man barked back.

Thinking he misunderstood, Rosalynn repeated her request.

He blurted a louder "No!"

We looked at each other and burst into laughter—lots of laughter. "I always wondered what I would do, if someone told me no!" she gasped.

Rosalynn has a sense of humor, and it stands her in good stead. No journalist or press reporter has described Rosalynn as being funny—but she is! Her view of an incident is often quite unusual, and when she airport marked a fundamental shift in the presidential campaign of 1976.

From Charlotte we went to Greenville, Columbia, Anderson, and Aiken, South Carolina, flying directly from Aiken to the Americus, Georgia, airport, ten miles out of Plains, where the first victory celebration was waiting.

On our arrival in Plains, a huge crowd of friends and supporters were waiting to cheer the victors. These hometown supporters celebrated every primary victory. I was planning to drive to Florida immediately, to be with my father again. But there was a message for me, saying it would be morning before Lucie could come to Plains with my car, so Miss Allie, Rosalynn's mother, asked me to spend the night at her house.

Early the next morning, a deeply shaken Beverly called to say that my father had died at 3:00 A.M. Beverly, who loved my father dearly, felt the loss as keenly as I did.

Miss Allie was wonderful. With her ability to instill calm and impart warmth in the midst of a crisis, she was a great comfort to me after Beverly's call, driving me to the Americus airport and giving me quiet words of comfort and assurance. Beverly had arranged for a private plane to take me to Florida. A few days later, on February 28, 1976, my father was buried in Calhoun, Georgia, after a simple graveside service.

While we were in Florida making plans to go to Calhoun for the funeral, Rosalynn called and said, "Edna, why didn't you call me? I feel as though I ought to be with you. I'll come to Calhoun." I had left Plains early in the morning. Since I knew the Carters were exhausted, I had not called them. I also knew how much was scheduled for Rosalynn and how important those few days to be with Amy and have some rest were for her, so I assured her things would be all right and persuaded her to keep to the schedule. I knew she would come if I needed her; that was enough.

My sister, Carol Boulukos, of Boston, was still with my mother in Florida after our father's funeral. We drove to Tampa, to attend a Carter rally and fish fry and to give Carol an opportunity to see Rosalynn and Jimmy the Sunday before the Florida primary.

The fish fry and rally at Lowry Park in Tampa brought together a huge crowd of Carter followers from all over the state. I have attended dozens of fish fries, but none compares with that Tampa event. Jimmy Carter's people smelled victory, and they pulled out all the stops. The decorated donkey and the green and white bunting were the trappings of victory, even though the primary election was still two days away. After the program, Rosalynn, Jimmy, and company boarded for the motorcade back to the airport. My son Jim had asked me to follow the entourage to the airport, so he could ride on the staff bus. As the motorcade moved out, I fell in near the end of the line. The scene was impressive. We had a police escort, four or five automobiles, motorcycles, and two buses, one for press and one for staff.

Pulling into the airport, we found two large aircraft—both Carter planes! Waving from the steps of one plane was Betty Rainwater. Boarding the other were Hamilton and Jody, with a large contingent of press.

Supporters from Iowa, New Hampshire, and other states had come to Florida to add their efforts in the final drive for a Florida win. Before the primaries were over, we would see many of these people over and over again.

All of this was quite a contrast to one year before almost to the day, when Rosalynn and I drove into Tampa in her car, unannounced and unknown! It dawned on me what was happening, and I was impressed.

My sister went home to Boston, and I stayed in Florida with my mother, helping her tend to the details and business surrounding my father's death.

Those were difficult days for me. I was saddened and tired. The Florida papers kept predicting that Jackson would win and that Humphrey would be drafted into the race. My own tattered emotions, combined with the negative press releases about Jimmy's campaign and the fact that recently I had not been as involved, gave me the only uneasiness I experienced in the entire campaign. I need not have worried; Jimmy won in Florida.

As Tuesday, March 9, 1976, came, I felt compelled to go to Orlando for the primary returns. Lucie and Jim were there, and Mother agreed to go with me and spend the night. Jack had campaigned hard in Florida, and as the day of the primary came, he decided to go home to Calhoun, to be with Jason and Judy. What a victory that was—unbelievable, yet real. It was happening. We were doing it—together.

*   *   *   *

On a Saturday night in early April, after I had been back in Calhoun from Mother's only three days, Rosalynn called and said, "Edna, I need describes it in her animated way with her gestures, we often end up in uncontrollable laughter!

One afternoon, on a handshaking walk in Van Buren, Maine, Rosalynn and I were on opposite sides of a street, going in and out of stores, handing out brochures, and inviting people to a 3:00 o'clock reception. The snow was piled high, and though we had on layers of clothes, the Maine air was very cold. As I walked into a little restaurant to hand out brochures and enjoy the warmth, a French-speaking customer offered to buy one of the brochures. *Ah, here was an opportunity to make use of my little bit of French.* I explained as best I could the purpose of my mission, while the customer listened "in his best English." Result? He still insisted on paying $3.00 for the brochure. I refused. He insisted. I refused.

While Rosalynn continued to campaign, I went to Sun City Center, Florida, to see about my father, who had been hospitalized following an automobile accident. Though apparently not serious in itself, the accident triggered other complications. My anxiety mounted as I visited him in that cold, sterile, intensive-care unit. However, after several days at his bedside, with the assurances from the doctors that he was better, I went back to New Hampshire to rejoin Rosalynn and the campaign.

As primary Election Day neared, family members, the Peanut Brigade, and other friends from around the country converged on New Hampshire for the final big drive. Our efforts paid off. The evening of February 24, Rosalynn, Jimmy, and a host of other supporters who had congregated in Manchester, celebrated a history-making victory. In the New Hampshire ice and snow, the Carters took another giant step toward the White House.

If we thought the New Hampshire win would give us a breather, we were mistaken. Those days following the New Hampshire primary vote are a blur—a painful blur—for me.

On the platform during the celebration of the New Hampshire victory, Rosalynn asked me to fly to South Carolina with her, to campaign on the way home. When we stopped in Charlotte, North Carolina, a large group of enthusiastic supporters greeted Rosalynn, presented her a huge bouquet of roses and the keys to the city, and hosted an impromptu reception. The crowd at the airport was thrilling, driving home to all of us the full impact of the incredible New Hampshire vote. I believe, in retrospect, that the appearance of the North Carolina supporters at the you." In some ways, the wins in New Hampshire and Florida had led me to believe it was all over. Not so! Rosalynn continued, "I really need to have someone with me I know! Jimmy and I would like you to meet us in Washington, D.C., tomorrow, Sunday noon. From there we both go to Wisconsin. Can you come?"

In order to be in Washington by noon, I had to leave the Atlanta airport on the early bird flight at 6:00 A.M., which meant leaving Calhoun at 4:00 A.M. But I was ready to go. As we boarded the chartered plane for Wisconsin, Rosalynn inquired, "What are we going to do in La Crosse?"

I laughed. I did not know we were *going* to La Crosse. All I had heard was Milwaukee. There was a large crowd at the La Crosse airport. With obvious relish, Jimmy bounded down the steps of his campaign plane and quickly moved to the crowds along the fence, shaking hands and giving them his increasingly famous grin. Rosalynn followed suit. She moved to the opposite end of the fence and greeted people, until she and Jimmy met in the middle of the fence.

After Jimmy's speech in La Crosse, we flew on to Milwaukee for the night. Rosalynn and Jimmy had a VIP suite, complete with fruits and cheeses and all kinds of fancy refreshments. Rosalynn said with a smile, "This is different from my first trip."

On the previous Friday, Rosalynn had stayed in the same hotel, with a little different service. As she prepared for bed that night, the desk clerk called to tell her that she would have to pay for her room in advance— *before* she went to sleep. Startled, she dressed quickly and went downstairs to pay. She handed the clerk a credit card.

"No!"

She handed the clerk a check.

"No!" The clerk demanded, "Cash only!"

Rosalynn had enough money to pay for the room, but she saw it would take nearly all her cash. Then she became angry. "I'm going to leave!"

"How soon? I'll send for your luggage," the clerk retorted.

Fortunately, just before they came to a parting of the ways, someone came to her rescue, assured the clerk that she was indeed Mrs. Jimmy Carter and that her credit card was good. No doubt the desk clerk has had many second thoughts since *that* night. On her second visit to the hotel a delicious dinner was served in Rosalynn and Jimmy's room. All was forgiven!

The next weeks of campaigning held some of our most unforgettable moments, some of which we would *like* to forget.

At Lancaster Square, Pennsylvania, we spent an hour or so in the Amish farmers' market, meeting people and examining some of the marvelous products of Lancaster. Altogether, we spent four or five hours in Lancaster, seeming to make good friends for Jimmy. Later, Mr. Charlie Smith, from Americus, Georgia, pointed out that Democrats were as scarce in Lancaster as Republicans in Americus, Georgia. That's *scarce!*

Rosalynn went back to Plains to spend Easter with her family. My brother, my mother, and I converged on my sister's house in Boston. Rosalynn came to Boston on Monday evening, to attend three separate fund-raising receptions in downtown Boston. We were to spend the night in the home of Tony and Hazel Scalli, in a historic Charlestown townhouse across the cobblestone street from the Paul Revere monument.

Rosalynn rode in the front seat of the Scallis' new two-door Chrysler with Tony. Hazel and I were in the back. When we stopped, Rosalynn could not get out of the car. "I can't get the seat belt unfastened," she said, puzzled. After doing everything we knew to do, she was still trapped. There was no other solution but to get scissors and cut the seat belt.

Inside, we found that many of the downtown guests had stopped by to say good night.

Around 10:00 P.M., someone asked me to come upstairs. I assumed that marked the end of the evening, since we had to get up at 5:00 A.M. But as I walked into the bedroom, Rosalynn was sitting on the bed, making a list. She looked up and said, "I don't know if I can wear these shoes for two weeks!" She spoke calmly, and I wondered why she thought she had to wear those shoes for two weeks.

The young woman from Carter headquarters, who had collected our luggage, declared, "Oh! Mrs. Langford doesn't know. We haven't told her yet!"

Then Rosalynn explained. "Our luggage is gone. It was stolen from the car. All the clothes we have are what we have on!"

In stunned disbelief, I blurted out, "Oh, but it couldn't be!"

Rosalynn quickly assured me that it was so. "Everything," she said, "including my wig." She had a wig so much like her own hair and hairstyle that I couldn't tell when she had it on. It was perfect for a quick television show and other impromptu appearances. But it was gone, too.

Rosalynn continued to make the list of all she had lost. After taking stock, we discovered we had only our briefcases (which had been left by our staff at the last reception, and had to be retrieved!), one coat, one extra pair of stockings between us, and our makeup. The only jewelry left was a gold necklace and a gold cross on a chain that I was wearing.

What do you do when something is stolen? You go to the police; so while Rosalynn got ready for bed—her day had started much earlier than mine—I made a visit to the police station, to make a report.

The final event of the evening continued to follow the pattern. As Rosalynn turned on the water to take a bath, the lovely crystal-and-gilt faucet fell apart!

Our hostess saved the night by lending us nightgowns and robes. Someone else provided hot curlers, body lotion (why body lotion?), and a small overnight case for Rosalynn. That's all we had when we left Boston for Pittsburgh at 6:00 the next morning.

Rosalynn had one day of campaigning in Pennsylvania before leaving for California. While she made a speech at a Beaver County Ramada Inn, I located some shoes for her to try on. Mary Narrish, campaigning with us as a Jimmy Carter delegate, helped pick out a black skirt for me. Snatching a moment together, Rosalynn and I walked through the large shopping mall, handing out brochures as we went. We stopped at a junior dress shop and bought her a blue short-sleeved sweater, a beige wraparound skirt, a blue scarf, and a half-slip—all for $29.41 (Rosalynn won't let me forget the change). Then she left, to go to California, Louisiana, and Indiana.

In all the pictures I saw of Rosalynn on the California trip, she wore the same outfit and looked good. Each night she stayed with friends who loaned her a nightgown and washed out her clothes Annette says that anytime Rosalynn sees a picture of herself wearing those clothes, she says, "I look like a cheerleader."

Rosalynn's California trip was without incident, except for one briefly embarrassing moment on the way back. In a Louisiana TV station, she was approached by a famous movie star who said, "I have traveled all

over the country for Jimmy and feel good about what is happening."
Rosalynn, having no idea who he was but appreciating his enthusiasm,
looked at him and asked, "And *who* are *you*?" so she could tell Jimmy
about him. With that, George Peppard introduced himself!

In Aliquippa, Pennsylvania, we visited the famous Church in the
Round, after spending the night with its pastor, the Reverend Elder
Clark and his wife, Melissa. With us were Mowry Mike, a volunteer from
Aliquippa, and David Doak, from our staff. There was no doubt we were
among friends who supported and encouraged us. As Rosalynn moved
to the platform to speak, I sensed she felt acceptance and gleaned
strength from the moment, as I did. She talked with the congregation
about Jimmy's longstanding appreciation and friendship with black people. She told them that years ago, when Billy Graham wanted to show
one of his films in Americus to an integrated audience, only Jimmy
Carter would assume chairmanship of the program. Rosalynn expressed
her deep feelings regarding the rights of all human beings. I was so glad
we had the opportunity to worship with them and that she had the
opportunity to speak.

Rosalynn arranged for Amy to accompany us to Indiana. We attended
a reception at Indiana Central University. Amy, though only eight, had
learned the ways of campaigning. She wandered around while we talked,
but always stayed close enough so that we never had to look or wait for
her.

As we made our way through the crowd at the university, a large
blond-haired man moved toward Rosalynn. Looming over her, he said
in a loud voice, "I don't like Jimmy Carter! I don't like you, either!" My
heart stopped. For a minute I was afraid. Then he produced a paper and
pencil and said, "But my mother wants your autograph!" Rosalynn
happily signed the man's paper for his mother.

In the middle of this meeting, word spread gradually among the crowd
that a bomb threat had been received. Everyone grew quiet and moved
quickly, in good order, toward an exit. As we went out the door, we saw
Amy was already outside, waiting for us, calm as a Carter.

The primaries rolled by. The steamroller effect continued. State after
state joined in celebrating a Carter victory—Illinois, Wisconsin, Pennsylvania, and finally Ohio. In spite of losses in California and some other
states with small delegate totals, Jimmy and Rosalynn were winning.

13

Icing On the Cake

A LOVE FEAST: That's what some commentators called the 1976 Democratic National Convention. It was a confirmation, a celebration. As the delegates gathered in New York City, there was really no way Jimmy could be denied the nomination. His eighteen victories out of thirty primaries had all but assured him of nomination. Jimmy's choice of a running mate held the only suspense, the only surprise, for the convention. With the exception of the defeated presidential candidates and their most devoted followers, delegates and visitors were ecstatic as they poured into New York in that early July. If they were not all Carter fans, they knew the White House was once again within the grasp of the Democratic Party. They would rally behind the former Georgia governor and his army of new faces. Jimmy would lead them back into power. For the most part, deep differences were covered over, buried, laid aside for the sake of party unity—a characteristic missing among Democrats since the terribly devisive Chicago convention of 1968.

Jimmy and Rosalynn came to the New York convention practically assured of the nomination because of significant changes in election laws brought into effect during the early 1970s. Especially after Watergate, election codes were rewritten to give the electorate an even greater role, not only in the general election, but in candidate selection. The wheeling and dealing among the power brokers in the back rooms at national party conventions had been curtailed. Under the new rules, candidates presented themselves to state caucuses and primaries, where delegates would be elected, pledged to one contender or another. Though regulations varied from state to state, the process was restored to the people. Presidential hopefuls had to push through the exhausting but crucial grass-roots delegate-selection process, if they would receive the coveted nomination. Vast amounts of money and incredible outlays of time were expended to insure that the American people regained control of the elections.

To go through the labyrinth of delegate selection demanded complete dedication by the candidate and his staff. However, as the election of 1976 came into sight, a full field of hopefuls lined up, eager for the contest. In addition to Jimmy Carter, other Democratic primary candidates were Morris Udall, George Wallace, Fred Harris, Frank Church, Milton Shapp, Henry Jackson, Birch Bayh, and Ellen McCormack. Some, like Jimmy, had been running for at least twelve months prior to the late fall of 1975, when they and several Republican candidates, including Gerald Ford and Ronald Reagan, officially began the drive for their party's nomination. Each one declared he would stay in the race until his party's convention. As a matter of fact, except for Morris Udall, Frank Church, and Jimmy Carter, one after another of the initial Democratic candidates dropped out, for one reason or another. Jerry Brown entered the race late and won some primaries, causing the Carters some concern. But he was actually never a threat, though he went to the convention making noises like a candidate with a chance.

The last few weeks of the primary season were the worst. Jimmy, the clear front-runner, became the target of the remaining candidates— especially Udall, Church, and Brown. Would Jimmy be able to hold and continue to pick up delegates and clinch the nomination? Yes! Ohio's June 8 primary unofficially assured Jimmy of the nomination. Udall, Church, even perennial candidate George Wallace—all but Jerry Brown —conceded that Jimmy had won the race.

Exhausted but jubilant, Jimmy and Rosalynn went home to Plains to celebrate and relax for a few days. After a short rest, Jimmy plunged into the process of binding up wounds inflicted by the bruising primary battles and selecting his running mate.

Because the nomination was essentially his, Jimmy, unlike most candidates before him, could devote careful attention to the selection of a vice-presidential running mate. Hamilton Jordan, Charles Kirbo, Jody Powell, and others on the staff drew up a list of names, with full dossiers on each one. Senators Muskie, Mondale, Glenn, Church, and Jackson, along with Congressmen Rodino and Adams and New York City Mayor Abe Beame, were seriously considered. By the time of the convention, Jimmy had narrowed his choice to Mondale, Muskie, and Glenn, but would tell no one how he really felt about a final selection.

Rosalynn was keenly interested in the nominees and made a point to be in some of the preliminary meetings Jimmy had with the potential candidates. As they came to Plains, she spent time with the men and their wives, but when Jimmy closeted himself with the hopefuls, Rosalynn left them alone. "Jimmy and I talked about the men and their wives, but I knew the decision had to be his. I had my ideas and told him, but Jimmy made the decision on his own," Rosalynn says.

The second week of July, 1976, found New York steamy, but ready to absorb the thousands who came from everywhere to take part in Jimmy's triumph. Modern American history has not seen a convention quite like the New York version. Though Jimmy and Rosalynn felt the victory was theirs already, they consistently refused to act like victors. The decision was not yet final. But their supporters had no such restraints. Parties, celebrations, and congratulations characterized the days in New York. Everyone thoroughly enjoyed the convention, claiming for Jimmy and for themselves a well-earned victory.

For me, an overriding memory of the convention is the way people moved from place to place: from the Americana Hotel to Madison Square Garden, from parties to luncheons, receptions to rallies in all parts of the city.

Rosalynn and Jimmy were not involved in this human traffic flow. They were already beginning to feel the restrictions of the office that soon would be theirs. But the rest of us were free. For each event, we met in front of the hotel, and boarded the Carter family bus together.

Excitement and anticipation made the chatter lively and noisy. Ever present media people added to the hurly-burly mood, especially when

Billy Carter entertained us with his impromptu, down-home-Georgia, country-boy fare. Another laugh for us was the contrast between our bus (its practicality stood symbolic of our candidate) and the long, black, chauffeured limousines that pulled in around us at the Garden!

One particular trip, which left a new and strange impression on me, was our visit to the zoo. Jack and Judy wanted to take one-year-old Jason. We certainly didn't anticipate the people's response to our visit. Groups gathered, word spread, and finally *we* became the zoo. Jack had to set Jason inside the fence with the ducks, because the press of the crowd had completely blocked him from our view. Then I realized fully that Jason's life would not be the same for a long, long time.

This new feeling about the way all our lives were changing continued as I joined Rosalynn for a luncheon. During those days, we had not had much time together. When I met her, she said, "Where have you been? I've seen so little of you, and I've needed you." It is hard to describe how fast events happened and how much was compressed into that one week. Of course, there were still some final assignments for party candidates to perform.

Preceding the luncheon, Rosalynn and I went to the Metropolitan Museum of Art, where she stood at the railing on the red-carpeted mezzanine and spoke to a large crowd of people gathered below. Watching her, I thought, *This is New York City! This is the convention! We've climbed for eighteen months. She doesn't look any different. I feel the same. But here we are!*

From my vantage point, the only peace and quiet at the convention was in Jimmy and Rosalynn's suite. Calmness prevailed behind those heavy doors.

Probably the major winner during that week was the security system, which made it hard for us to see our visiting friends from all over the country. The size of the convention floor, where state delegations and their alternates were seated, prevented general distribution of convention floor passes. A limited number of Carter family passes was made available by the Democratic National Committee for entrance to the convention floor. (Sometimes we lost sight of the fact that there were *other* candidates at the convention with family, supporters, and staff from over the country as well!)

On Monday night, waiting our turn for a family pass, Emily Dolvin

(Aunt Sissy who is Miss Lillian's youngest sister), Ralph Snyder (my brother I call Buddy), and I watched from a perch high in the gallery. Suddenly, the section we were sitting in became deserted. Ushers finally came to escort Sissy, Buddy, and me into another area until a mysterious briefcase on the floor behind us was examined. It was a bomb scare!

Tuesday night, after using all of our persuasive powers on young staff people who were unaware of the scope of Sissy's and my campaign travels, we cajoled floor passes. The evening found Sissy and me in the midst of one of our happiest moments of the convention. Down on the convention floor, weaving from state to state, section to section, among the friends that were almost like family, we enjoyed reunion after reunion. Rosalynn wanted to be there, but security and protocol wouldn't permit it, so she said, "Tell them I would come myself, if I could—and how I *wish* I could. Tell them how much we appreciate what they have done!" More than one excited, emotionally moved person met this message with tears in their laughter as they hugged me or Sissy, sending real love and appreciation back to Jimmy and Rosalynn. More than one said —solemnly and with reverence in the midst of all the revelry—"God bless them. God bless them." Like Rosalynn, I do not cry often, but I cry even now, as I remember and write this.

Listening to all the stories that stemmed from the celebration activities, one particulary appeals to me.

Cathy Rogers, a member of the staff, who worked closely with Rosalynn and me in New Hampshire, voiced the opinion of most staff workers gathered in New York when she said, "All the ridicule we suffered for supporting such an unknown candidate came to nothing, the minute the deciding delegate vote was cast. For us, the convention was one big party, the icing on the cake!"

While delegates and supporters were in hotels all over town, the Americana, on Fifty-second Street and Seventh Avenue, had been named the official hotel. Jimmy and Rosalynn were in a lovely, large suite on the twenty-first floor, protected from potential enemies (as well as family and friends) by incredibly tight security. In fact, the wall of security that necessarily surrounded the Carters had a net effect of sealing off many close friends and family, creating anger and frustration. Even VIPs had to subject themselves to close Secret Service checks before they could enter the double oak doors into the suite.

When balloting began on Tuesday night, four names were placed in nomination: Morris Udall, Edmund Gerald (Jerry) Brown, Ellen McCormack (an anti-abortion candidate), and Jimmy Carter. Udall finally released his delegates to Jimmy. Amid the happy, celebratory noise of Madison Square Garden, the roll call began. At 11:16 P.M., Ohio, the state that clinched his nomination in June, made it official in July: Jimmy Carter, of Plains, Georgia, would be the presidential candidate for the Democratic Party. The scene in the Carter suite is firmly etched in my mind. Jimmy was hemmed in by a small crowd of well-wishers, while Rosalynn moved around the room, speaking to everyone.

Miss Lillian, already dressed in her long, flowing, peach colored robe, said to everyone and no one, "Everybody, please go to bed!" She had had enough adventure for one day! But her feelings were not shared by those in the room. Most were far too excited to even think of going to bed.

Looking back, the months between the Democratic National Convention and the general election on November 4 seem like a blink of the eye, a snap of the fingers. The days came and went; campaigning was over. Decision time was upon us. Some worried: "What will we do, if we lose?"

Jimmy's response was firm: "I don't have to be president. I can go home to Plains. I have my warehouse and my land and my home!"

Election Day, November 4, 1976, brought family and friends together again at Atlanta's Omni International Hotel and the World Congress Center.

Excitement outside the hotel and the World Congress Center reached such a pitch that passage through the streets was impossible. Virtually everyone had come. A late supper had been arranged for the 1976 Carter crowd, but now it was a bigger, more experienced team. The young campaigners had become seasoned veterans: our children were adults.

Everywhere, television sets were the center of attention. Statistics were noted, totals revised and compared. In Jimmy's suite, where two television sets sat side by side, eyes were riveted on the election results. Again, calm prevailed, but it was an excited calm as the drama was played out. Hamilton and Jody moved quickly back and forth from one connecting room to another, discussing the results, evaluating the trends. The usual table of food, coffee, and Coca-Colas stood hardly noticed. Furniture was pulled around, so that all had a view of the television sets. Rosalynn's sister Allethia and her husband, Lee Wall; Jimmy's sister Ruth and her husband, Bobby Stapleton; Miss Allie; Miss Lillian; Amy; Billy and Syble Carter; Nan Powell; Nancy Jordan—all came in and out. Charlie Kirbo, Jerry Rafshoon, and others always involved in the mechanics of Jimmy's campaigns appeared and disappeared, while Jimmy and Rosalynn—usually sitting by each other—watched and waited.

Beverly and I moved back and forth, from the Carters' room to Jack and Judy's room by the elevator. Discovering early that crossing the street to the convention hall was not possible, we satisfied ourselves with seeing those friends who made their way to the hotel. When news on Jack's television seemed inadequate or inconclusive, Beverly went back to check on the two sets in Jimmy's room. Everyone stuck to his post through midnight and on into the early morning hours.

The passage of time only seemed evident in the positions of the guests in the chairs and on the sofas in the candidate's suite. Ruth and Bobby Stapleton sat at the same end of the long sofa, where they intermittently watched and napped. Now others slumped, heads back, eyes closed, waiting. Except for the wide-awake presidential candidate and his First Lady-to-be, the scene reminded me of Walt Disney's *Sleeping Beauty,* when all the people in the land slept just where they were, until some magic awakened them!

And then, sometime after 3:00 A.M., the magic awakened us all—never to sleep the same again! Jimmy had won! It was certain. No more guessing, hoping it was a victory! Straightening hair and clothes, gathering up tote bags and overnight kits that would go to Plains with them, the family moved to the waiting automobiles that would drive them the 300 yards to the cavernous, teeming World Congress Center to claim Jimmy Carter's victory!

It is hard to record my feelings and thoughts as I stood on that platform behind Jimmy and Rosalynn, looking into a sea of unrecognizable faces. In looking back, I realize that there was little of the past to think about, given the enormity of what lay ahead.

Beverly and I caught a ride back across the still-crowded area to the hotel. November is creepy cold in Georgia, and we shivered with no wraps. Several young people had gathered in our rooms, so we fell into bed in the spacious, deserted presidential suite. Leaving the television in the bedroom on, so we would not miss any of the news from Plains, we napped for an hour or so. Then we watched Jimmy and Rosalynn meet their family and their lifelong friends at home. It was dawn as Jimmy said, "The sun is rising on a beautiful new day, and there is a beautiful new spirit in this country." All I can remember thinking at that time was, *What have we done to Jimmy and Rosalynn?*

The campaigning was over. But there was a lot of planning to be done. Rosalynn was concerned that all our old supporters be invited to attend the inaugural celebrations. Also, we had some shopping to do before January. I had the fun of choosing the material for Rosalynn's inaugural-day outfit. After much nervous deliberation, I chose a vivid, teal-blue wool. Then I tried on a dress in the proposed style and felt that Rosalynn would be pleased. Our usual luck held out! Inaugural-day pictures have that bright blue-green focal point wherever Rosalynn appeared. Brown boots from one of our favorite shoe salesman completed the outfit. Things were humming. There was an inauguration ahead.

14

Stepping Into History

CLANG. The sound of iron against concrete echoed as the manhole cover fell into place on Pennsylvania Avenue. The scene: Washington, D.C. The time: in the early morning hours of January 22, while it was still dark. Each manhole cover was removed and the exposed tunnel examined by a United States Secret Service agent. From that moment through the remaining part of the night, they stood guard along Pennsylvania Avenue.

Inauguration day, 1977, was at hand, and Jimmy Carter was to take the oath of office as the thirty-ninth President of the United States of America. A few days prior to the inauguration, Jimmy told Rosalynn and Chip (who was coordinating arrangements) that he had talked to the Secret Service about their walking back to the White House after the inaugural ceremony. It had never been done before. The Secret Service was nervous. They prepared for the occasion, but only on the condition that if the plan became known, it would have to be canceled.

The walk went on as planned. Down Pennsylvania Avenue they came, accepting the presidency in a unique way, representing the people, identifying with all the common folk of the land. Striding with a vigorous step and winsome spirit, hand in hand with the family that had inspired them, Jimmy and Rosalynn captured the hearts of Americans everywhere.

The days before the inauguration were not all glitter and glamour. We were all skeptical of the news-hungry press, searching for every snippet of news, representative of the type of treatment Jimmy would get, once he settled into the presidential routine. Newspaper readers' eyebrows lifted in shock when Rosalynn announced she would wear her six-year-old Georgia inaugural gown to the presidential inaugural ball. Would Amy's schooling become a *cause célèbre?* Would she go to public or private school? Who was Mary Fitzpatrick, and why was she coming to the White House? Is Miss Lillian Jimmy's mother or Rosalynn's mother? On and on, the press questioned and probed. It was a necessary hazard of those preinaugural days.

The day before the inauguration, after the busy weeks of the transition period, Rosalynn and Jimmy came to Washington. At President Ford's invitation, they stayed in Blair House, across Pennsylvania Avenue from the White House. By now, every movement was a ceremony: motorcade, police escorts, scurrying photographers and television cameramen, and crowds of people lining the routes.

That evening, the inaugural gala was held at the Kennedy Center, with entertainers like Beverly Sills, Loretta Lynn, and Redd Foxx performing for the guests. It was a fun evening—almost like an escape for Rosalynn and Jimmy. She told me later that it was so good to be able to avoid the spotlight for a few hours. That night was really family night for the Carters. All of Rosalynn's brothers and sisters were there, too: Allethia, who calls Rosalynn "Sister" and is eleven years younger, and her husband, architect Lee Walls; Gerald Smith and his wife, Ino, from Pittsburgh; and Murray Smith, teacher and coach from Sumter County.

*   *   *   *

Inauguration day, 1977: inches of snow on top of snow, glistening under a high, bright winter's sun beaming across the rolling hills of the city. The graceful Potomac had stopped in its tracks, frozen solid, taking a holiday, like millions of others in the country.

In keeping with their religious commitments, Rosalynn and Jimmy encouraged, but were unable to attend, a morning prayer service at the Lincoln Memorial. Thousands willingly faced the chill of the early hours to start the day of inaugural celebration with worship. Martin Luther King, Senior, on the spot where his martyred son once stood, delivered a stirring prayer-sermon from John 21 for the new president and the nation he would lead. With deep emotion, he said, "The sheep must be fed. . . . Martin Luther King gave his life that the best of them may never be forgotten. . . . That's what the president-elect is all about." Tall, angular, strikingly beautiful Leontyne Price banished the cold with "He's Got the Whole World In His Hand," and finally a stately looking black man, forever anonymous but forever remembered, raised his bare hand toward the sky in eloquent but unspoken benediction over all assembled.

At 9:00 A.M. on inaugural day, the Carter family, Vice-President and Mrs. Mondale, and approximately fifty guests assembled at First Baptist Church of Washington for a private time of worship and commitment. It was a moment of gathering together, of being grateful for the days gone by, and a time of commitment to the days ahead—a silent covenant to pray for one another. Here I felt the intimacy of the friendship developed over our years of nurturing a single purpose together.

Rosalynn and Jimmy began this special day in worship. They felt the need to begin the term of office in reliance upon God and with prayers for strength and guidance in the days ahead. The remainder of this special day was going to be public; they wanted to begin it in the privacy of God's house.

At the United States Capitol, we in the family, with some special friends, were seated in a reserved section on the inaugural platform. Even though I was seated several yards from Rosalynn and Jimmy, I could see them clearly. The ceremony began with Bishop Cannon's powerful invocation.

As the inaugural ceremony proceeded, my mind raced back from this moment of glory to those days of anonymity, when we traveled together to Florida, to New Hampshire, to Maine and all the other places. We had always believed this day would come, but now it *had* arrived, I had an extraordinary feeling of calm. While drinking it all in, tucking the sights and sounds and feelings away in safe corners of my mind, from where I could later extract and savor them, I was struck with my own lack of awe. I was not overwhelmed by it all, and what's more, I was sure that Rosalynn was equally taking it all in stride. I had prevailing sense

of good. This was right. Jimmy and Rosalynn were the right people for
this moment in our history: God's people, our people. Awe? No, but a
deep sense of gratitude for them and for the goodness of our relationship.

Then James Earl Carter, with Rosalynn by his side, was standing
under the simple inaugural-stand portico, silhouetted against the white
snow. With the Capitol dome towering overhead; with thousands of
people from across the nation standing in the snow, some even perched
in the trees; Chief Justice Warren Burger asked Jimmy if he were prepared to take the oath of office. Jimmy responded positively and placed
his hand on the Bible that had been given to him a few years before by
his mother. The Bible was opened to Micah 6:8: "He hath shewed thee,
O man, what is good; and what doth the Lord require of thee, but to do
justly, and to love mercy, and to walk humbly with thy God?" As Jimmy
took the oath, " . . . President of the United States . . . ." I had to
silently mouth the phrase, to let it sink in.

From where I sat, they looked so small—almost diminutive—so tiny,
with such a big world to hold together. And yet they loomed larger than
the office, because I knew they were not alone! I had a deep assurance
of God's being present with them at that moment, and prayed that it
would always be so.

When Rosalynn speaks of standing by Jimmy as his hand was on the
Bible, she says, "I can't remember a particular feeling I had as we stood
there. I looked at all the people and knew we had a responsibility to
them. I looked at Jimmy and knew he was capable, and I knew that he
wanted this country to be moral and good. But all at once the enormity
of the position zoomed in on me. The world responsibility was something
I had not realized. We wanted our country to have standing and position,
so that all other countries would look at us and be proud! I felt the heavy
responsibility that Jimmy would have—even in the midst of all the
excitement."

Then came Jimmy's address. My mind and eyes wandered over to
Rosalynn, and for a moment—just a moment—I stopped listening to
Jimmy and thought, *What a good choice that color was!* I smiled, thinking
about the trauma I went through getting Rosalynn's comfortable boots!
They had to be comfortable, to walk that mile.

Then I was listening to Jimmy again:

Here before me is the Bible used in the inauguration of our first president in 1789, and I have just taken the oath of office on the Bible my mother gave me just a few years ago, opened to a timeless admonition from the ancient prophet Micah . . .

You have given me a great responsibility—to stay close to you, to be worthy of you, and to exemplify what you are. Let us create together a new national spirit of unity and trust. Your strength can compensate for my weakness, and your wisdom can help to minimize my mistakes. . . .

Within us, the people of the United States, there is evident a serious and purposeful rekindling of confidence. And I join in the hope that when my time as your president has ended, people might say this about our nation:

that we had remembered the words of Micah. . . .

that we had strengthened the American family,
  which is the basis of our society. . . .

that we had enabled our people to be proud
  of their own government once again. . . .

I remember hoping he would not pause in the wrong place while he gave his speech. His manner was so easy—informal, and yet pointed. In his steady, measured address, he set the tone for an administration studiously shorn of the imperial, designed to lead us, to reaffirm the cornerstones of American life—simplicity, self-reliance, love for peace, commitment to human rights, faith in one another, and faith in God.

And there were Gerald and Mrs. Ford. At one time or another, most of us know what it is to lose, but few will suffer the pain of losing control of the highest office in the land. Jimmy chose his words carefully. How gracious of him to recognize Mr. Ford's role: "I want to thank my predecessor for all he has done to heal our land." Then they began their walk.

From our seats in the parade reviewing stand, I could see Rosalynn and Jimmy coming up the street. We shared a secret: Rosalynn was wearing a gold neck chain and a small antique gold cross that belonged to me. It is an heirloom I have worn for a long time. Rosalynn had worn it before, and loved it. We had added two other crosses to the chain, especially for that occasion. The first cross was for Jason, then our only grandchild. To capture the day in a symbolic manner, we added two new gold crosses, heirlooms-to-be—one for Amy and one for Chip's and Caron's yet unborn child. We planned to pass on to our children and our children's children a bit of the heart of our friendship.

I guessed by now Rosalynn was numb, not only from the cold, but because everything was happening so fast. Later, she said it reminded her of Thornton Wilder's play, *Our Town*. In one part, Emily, who has died, asks to go back to her hometown for one day, to relive her twelfth birthday. As Emily walks around and looks at everyone, she says, "It goes so fast. Why don't they stop and look at each other?"

Rosalynn's feelings that day were the same. She said, "The day went so quickly. The activities swirled around me. I had no time to speak or say thank-you to people anywhere." She saw friends and family among the crowds lining the street, but she could only wave her hand. She told me later, "I wanted to touch each person and say, 'This is the beginning. It is for you and will be for you. Please help us. Please pray for us.' And as I looked at Jimmy, I thought, *This is where you belong. You can do a good job for our country. I know you are right for this place.* But there was so little time."

As the inaugural parade neared its conclusion, I noticed Jody and Nan Powell and their daughter Emily leaving their seats in the reviewing stands and making their way toward the gate of the White House grounds. The guard at the gate did not yet know of all the president's senior staff, so Jody had to present his identification to gain entrance. The front lawn and driveway were cast in late-afternoon shadows. As Jody walked toward the mansion between his wife and daughter, he slipped an arm around each of them, hesitated a moment, seemed to look up at the White House, took a deep breath, and walked into the front door of the mansion—and into history. It strikes me that Jody, Nan, and Emily took that walk for all of us. All of us entered a completely new phase of our lives that day.

For more than two hours that frosty afternoon, we watched bands (including the Calhoun High School band!), floats, marching units, horses: the inaugural parade. As we watched, we stirred around to ward off the penetrating cold, laughed, and visited with family and friends. It was a delirious afternoon for Rosalynn and Jimmy and for millions of us in the country who worked and gave and prayed that he might become our president. As the shadows lengthened, the last unit strutted past the president's reviewing stand, we turned to go into the White House—to go home with President and Mrs. Carter!

In January, 1971, when Rosalynn first drove onto the grounds of the Georgia governor's mansion as a resident and entered the stately, columned house, her first words were, "I can't believe it!" The move from Plains to Atlanta, from the work in the warehouse to the work in the governor's mansion, was Rosalynn's *giant* step. From that moment on, Rosalynn and Jimmy belonged to the people.

Now, as she walked into the White House for the first time as a resident, Rosalynn felt a deep feeling of satisfaction and accomplishment. It was the culmination of the conviction she had experienced for months. Remember the incident on the plane, looking out over the city of Chicago? Oh, there was excitement and wonder, but above all there was the emotion of acceptance: acceptance of responsibility and leadership. She and Jimmy had talked about—had dreamed about—the moment for so long. When Jimmy's election was certain, she had said to me, "Now we can do anything!"

The world saw the Carters dance together at the inaugural balls held in several locations in Washington. "Ladies and gentlemen," the voice blared over the public-address system, "the President of the United States and Mrs. Carter." A tumultuous greeting went up from the elegantly gowned and handsomely dressed throng at the Washington National Guard Armory, as the spotlight picked up a smiling and waving Rosalynn and Jimmy coming into the hall. Slowly, they made their way through the crowd of well-wishers to the stage. Then, while Guy Lombardo played "The Sweetest Music This Side of Heaven," the president and First Lady did several graceful turns amid the cheers of an admiring audience.

Beverly and I, along with other family members, moved in through the crowd for a while and then made our way up to a balcony reserved for family and special guests. In the soft light of the armory, I could pick out friends from Florida, Georgia, New Hampshire, Iowa, Oklahoma, and dozens of other states Rosalynn and I had visited. A profound sense of satisfaction stole through me. Indeed, it had been worth it all.

* * * *

The next day, Carter Innkeepers were invited to the White House, and what a gorgeous White House it was. In recognition of Rosalynn's love for flowers and gardening, women from the garden clubs of Georgia had transformed every room into a spring garden of Georgia flowers. Where in the world did they get all those flowers in mid-January? There were camellias, azaleas, daisies, daffodils, and dozens and dozens of roses—all exquisitely arranged in big urns and exotic bowls. And the peaches! From somewhere, the resourceful decorators had found peaches and worked them into arrangements here and there. One particularly determined gardener brought a Georgia pine tree on the airplane to Washington, displayed it for the reception, then saw to its careful planting on the White House lawn.

From everywhere, the Innkeepers came: hundreds of men and women who had opened their homes and cupboards to the Carters and their campaigners during the long quest for the White House. This was their day.

Rosalynn and Jimmy stood in the State Hall under the great seal of the President of the United States, greeting everyone. Passing through the room behind her, I saw Rosalynn motioning for me. "Give me a Kleenex," she whispered. With tears brimming in her eyes, she said, "I was doing all right, until I saw them all here. Edna, they're all here! Just look over there." And she mentioned by name several who had just passed through the receiving line.

I handed her a tissue and thought, *Here we are in this big room, this big house with all these people, people who have never been here before and who would never have had this chance to come, if it had not been for Rosalynn and Jimmy. And Rosalynn and Jimmy would never have been here, if it had not been for them!*

Again I thought of that flight over Chicago and Rosalynn's comment. "Look at all those lights, representing all those people; people that we will be responsible for."

How does one describe any moment or day when everything comes together? How does one describe several moments: lived; enjoyed; shared; deep beyond words; quiet, even with a world looking on; and spiritual as the most moving religious experience?

How does one describe the realization of a moment worked for, dreamed of, imagined from every possible angle?

How does one find words or emotions to describe the meaning of a once-in-a-lifetime, once-in-the-history-of-mankind moment?

15

Sharing the Dream

What have we done to Rosalynn and Jimmy? That was the question that came to my mind on the night the election results indicated he would be President and she his First Lady. Behind that question was some anxiety, anticipation, and excitement. It made sense that they were going to lead the nation. It was exhilarating to think I had been a part of their steps toward the White House.

Thinking about my friend Rosalynn, I've never had any doubts about her ability to fulfill successfully the role of First Lady. In fact, a major reason for writing this book has been to share some insights about her and to give a fuller picture of Rosalynn, especially from the perspective of our friendship. I think most Americans are intrigued by this lady from Plains, Georgia.

At the time the Carters were leaving the Georgia governor's mansion at the end of Jimmy's term of office, a friend came by to wish them well as they went back to Plains. I was there when, as he was leaving, he stopped, turned around, and said to Rosalynn, "I'm glad you have not changed during these four years. You are the same person you were when you came here."

She thanked him graciously for his kind words. After he left, Rosalynn looked at me and said, "But how would I change?"

I could have said, "In many ways. It's not unusual for people who achieve a high public office to reject their roots or forget their friends, or adopt newfangled ideas and project their new status in life. . . ." But that's not Rosalynn. There has been change in her life. It can be seen in various ways: a greater knowledge of world affairs, more facility in public speaking, less time for herself. But there has been no change in her basic character or her perspective. Her priorities are the same.

Yes, she raises her voice sometimes. Yes, she gets mad at Jimmy. Yes, they disagree about issues. Yes, she gets discouraged. Yes, she does look at herself in a picture and say, "Why did I ever wear that?" Yes, she makes mistakes. Yes, she gets frustrated and says, "How can I get all this done when time is running out?" And yes, sometimes she says, "I don't like what the president did in that situation." She can be friendly, cold, kind, resolute, sweet, cross, happy, sad, lonely, confused, grateful—but always Rosalynn.

There are those who think, "The picture you've given of Rosalynn is a biased one, based on your mutual friendship." This is true, but she has other friends who have seen her at those same "real" times, when her feet hurt and she complained about them, or when she got up before dawn to roll her hair, make her bed, drink a quick cup of coffee, pack, and run. Many others were with her and know her, too.

Looking back over the years since 1966, when Jimmy's race for the Georgia governorship meshed all of our lives into a venture that carried us beyond the sphere of "let's make-believe," to the reality of today, I see us now as we were then: the same people. We're older, wiser, certainly more traveled, but the same people.

Fourteen years ago, Rosalynn Carter would have said, "I love what I am doing. I know Jimmy loves his work, too. We have a quiet peace and security in believing that what we are doing is right. I believe we are where we should be."

She says the same thing today.

Rosalynn believes that what she and Jimmy are doing for this country will have lasting significance. Perhaps some of their specific goals will not be accomplished, but she believes the tone and feeling they have sought to share with the people will remain. She knows many will not fully understand the spiritual base on which they operate, but there's a confidence that the world will not forget their emphasis on personal integrity, human rights, and justice for all people. That's Rosalynn.

It's so easy to view living in the White House as a glamour job. *What a plum,* some must think. In a sense, it's true. Rosalynn does not have to worry about leaky plumbing, ironing, and beauty-parlor appointments. She doesn't have to pick up the cleaning or systematically dust the house each day. But amid all the hustle and bustle, a First Lady's wardrobe does not magically appear, the perfect size and appropriate style for every occasion. The First Family's meals don't magically please special tastes, unless the wife and mother plans it that way.

Frustration is probably one of her closest companions. She has only twenty-four hours in her day, too. Thirty minutes to practice violin with Amy takes thirty minutes, and so she schedules this time. Does that sound strange and affected? Only because we are talking about the president's wife. You schedule your daughter's music lessons, too. I could go on and on, listing the responsibilities of each day, including the state dinners to be planned, the speeches to be written and given, the appearances to be made. And remember, much of this occurs in public.

Where does Rosalynn get the stamina? Self-discipline is the key.

To be able to hold up under the strain of an unrelenting schedule, she stays in good physical condition. She and Jimmy encourage each other to exercise and diet. Since coming to live in the White House, which has a kitchen noted for its excellent cuisine, and moving in the midst of a constant round of teas, receptions, and dinners, the Carters have had many opportunities to indulge. But they rarely eat at social events, primarily because they would rather speak to the guests. For lunch, Rosalynn regularly goes to the family dining room and has a salad plate. In Thailand, her good physical condition showed as she moved with vigor in wilting temperatures through the refugee camps at Sa Kaew.

When self-discipline combines with total involvement, however, my husband, Beverly, has accused us both of having tunnel vision. I once had a reputation for tardiness. That has improved. But Rosalynn always wants to be on time. I must admit, sometimes I have seen us "strain at a gnat and swallow a camel," trying to be on time when a five-minute delay would have saved an hour's wait later on. The wayward gypsy in my heart often leads me astray from schedules. Unfortunately, my conscience often indicates I would have done better to have stayed on track. Interestingly, when Rosalynn comes back from a Camp David weekend with a briefcase that has been unopened, she feels guilty, too.

Another of the common denominators in our friendship is our real curiosity about the things around us—close at home and way out there!

My daddy had an organization to which he daily appointed and reappointed officers. He called it the HTMAs. When I got particularly involved in wanting to find out about everything going on, he designated me as president of the HTMAs—the Hate to Miss Anythings! Rosalynn is always a member, and often an officer. And why not? She has a constant thirst for discovery and information. She doesn't try to know the minute details of everything, but she does want to know the overall position that Jimmy takes on many of the policies that affect her or her interests. Her note taking while she sits in on policy meetings is the result of a developed, intelligent curiosity. She wants to be informed and prepared to share viewpoints with Jimmy, to talk—express feelings—feel secure. All of us are able to grow when we feel secure. Self-confidence is the dividend of persistent study, reflection, and mutually appreciated interactions. This shows in Rosalynn's life.

It is true that Rosalynn has a deep, personal faith in God, and that this is the foundation of her life. Her faith, like most of ours, was sparked and nurtured in a church community. She would be quick to say, however, that her faith is not in the church, but in Jesus Christ. But like many of us who grew up in a small community, our faith was nurtured and developed in the confines of the local church. Not only were we taught about church doctrine and church structure and awakened to the needs of other people, but our social life was bound up in the church. When a new family moves into town, one of the first questions asked is, "What church do y'all go to?"—just that way!

In public, Rosalynn does not talk about her faith as easily or as often as Jimmy. But those of us who know her well see her faith expressing itself in deeds far more eloquent than words.

Through the years, Rosalynn and I have talked often about our religious faith and how it affects our attitudes and ideas of life. We've both been strengthened by these conversations. We've grown together. You have to grow, when you face the kinds of personal problems and the unique situations we have.

We've talked about negative feelings and our reactions to what happens to us. As problems occur, we have tried to put into practice this significant principle: "It's not what happens to you, but how you take it, that makes the difference."

We all know how difficult it is to forgive others. Rosalynn's fierce loyalty and her protective instincts make it almost impossible to forget and very difficult to forgive violators, when her family is involved. Sometimes, she's like the mama tiger with her cubs!

My husband's father, Otto Langford, had strong feelings, which could be especially provoked by unfairness, and he often had to work hard to forgive the offender. When he felt he could, he offered to "bury the hatchet." When it was particularly hard, he muttered, "But I'm leaving the handle sticking up!" I think sometimes Rosalynn has to leave the handle sticking up, too.

One other important principle I've learned from Rosalynn, or at least with her, relates to the matter of negatives and how we handle them. Sometime ago, Ginny Reese, my close friend for more than twenty years, who has known Rosalynn nearly as long as I have, said, "You and Rosalynn don't let things bother you. You do your best with problems, then you don't worry about them anymore." Each of us struggles in different ways to accomplish what we set out to do. Rosalynn struggles just like the rest of us. All of us hope that our struggles will help us as we grow and feel better about ourselves.

Jimmy and Rosalynn have a philosophy of history that grows out of their deep religious faith and frees them from undue burdens. They believe that God is ultimately in control of history, that He has a purpose for His creation that is larger than any nation or any era in history. Our responsibility is to discern what is moral and right, using our best efforts to do what we think God desires for His people. I can hear Rosalynn say it now: "We do our best, we work hard, we pay whatever price is necessary, and then we sleep soundly all night. God is in control of our history." This larger, biblical view provides them freedom and inspiration to labor hard and long, while still keeping their own lives in perspective.

Both Rosalynn's and Jimmy's families have deep roots in the Sumter County area. When Rosalynn joined the Carter family, she brought a great family heritage to the marriage; a heritage that gave her the stability, strength, and determination to find her own life as part of the often rough-and-tumble Carter clan.

It hasn't always been easy for Rosalynn. As a very young wife and mother, her navy life was different from life in a tiny south Georgia town. "With a population of six hundred eighty-three, everyone always knew everything about everybody in Plains!" But in Norfolk, Virginia, or Schenectady, New York, there was an anonymity—a privacy. When Jimmy was at home in those days, the demands on his time and Rosalynn's were made only by each other and the things they chose to do.

Rosalynn and Jimmy quickly found many common threads running through their lives. One of these was their need for privacy. So whether in a small town, the governor's mansion, the midst of a political campaign, or even in the White House, they carefully draw a circle of privacy around themselves. Their staffs know about this priority and are extremely reluctant to disturb the Carters after they go "home" to the family floor of the White House or to Camp David.

Another mutual need they have is for open, consistent communication. They have to talk with each other. Ideas, criticisms, suggestions are batted back and forth. They sharpen each other. When they are campaigning on separate trips, wherever they are in the course of a day, they frequently phone each other to compare notes, share news, and keep in touch.

Recently, when the news from Iran and other parts of the world was particularly distressing, Rosalynn left her office in the East Wing, walked over to the Oval Office, and said, "Jimmy, can we talk a few minutes?" And that's exactly what they did. For a few minutes, Jimmy and Rosalynn sat out on the secluded little terrace behind his office and talked. In a short while, Chip, who had been away campaigning, joined them. It was a private circle: a family talking. No major decisions were made, but expressions of care, of support, and of encouragement were voiced.

Not long ago, at a business luncheon, a man said to me, "I don't like what Rosalynn Carter is doing. I didn't elect her President of the United

States. I don't want *her* making the decisions."

For a minute, I was speechless. He didn't know Jimmy or Rosalynn. How do you explain their partnership? Surely he had misread Jimmy Carter. He couldn't possibly know the inner strength of the man, the will, the stubbornness that can be reflected in his steel-blue eyes. Decisions? Sure—every day there are decisions—and he makes them. She's part of him, however, and that's their strength. It's a partnership: a relationship in which they teach each other, communicate with each other, belong to each other's world.

This partnership, their private circle, also includes their family. They encourage their children to be involved with them—to be aware of what goes on—but they also encourage their children to live their own lives, to be as public or as private as they choose.

This commitment to let their children develop according to their own interests doesn't mean Jimmy and Rosalynn practice a hands-off policy. Both have been quick to express to the children opinions about college, occupations, places to live, running for public office, divorce, and religion. It is rare, indeed, when any of the Carter children don't know what their parents feel about a certain situation. But having given their opinion, Rosalynn and Jimmy know from their own experience that the children have to work out their own affairs.

Rosalynn makes herself available to the children and their families. At one time or another, all three boys and their wives have lived with Rosalynn and Jimmy. The White House and its functions are wide open to all three sons. For them, invitations are open to all special events.

As the boys have grown up, Rosalynn and Jimmy have adapted their relationship with their sons. Today they are friends with Jack, Chip, and Jeff, as well as being their parents. There have been times when one son or another has urged a certain course of action on Jimmy. Jimmy has felt free to do as he deemed best with their suggestions. Such exchanges of ideas or opinions, given and taken, are part of that private, family circle.

However, Jack says he more than likely would give his opinion only once to his father. His mother will make her point more often. Consequently, if a particular family problem comes along, the boys often sound Rosalynn out before they talk with Jimmy. The availability of Rosalynn's time and her listening nature draw the discussion to her first.

Also, the grandchildren are fast developing their own relationship with Rosalynn and Jimmy. They know "Mom" and "Pa-paw." Once, when Jason was looking out the window, he saw the helicopter land on the south lawn of the White House. As Jimmy stepped off the plane, he waved to the waiting crowd. For Jason, looking out the window, the wave was just for him. "Look, Pa-paw is waving at *me!*" With that, Jason pumped his little hand up and down and waved back.

Rosalynn has fitted in well with the Carter clan. She's added a dimension that has made its mark on all their lives. Her natural, quiet temperament and her disciplined control have produced a mystique that is not something gaudy or flamboyant, but challenging and arresting to those of us who know her.

Strangers have dissected her personality, her actions, and her motives. They have analyzed, judged, and recorded their opinions of our First Lady.

Kandy Stroud, a writer, terms the story of Rosalynn as "one of extraordinary personal growth accomplished with cast-iron willpower and the aid of her mate." That's an accurate perception.

In and out of some seventy airports, countless towns and cities in some thirty states (she made forty-one states), Rosalynn and I smiled and laughed and talked and walked and ran and made friends.

We've shared laughter and tears, good times and bad times, wins and losses, hurts and happinesses. We shared a common life-style, a common philosophy, a common faith. We believed in what we were saying and in what we were doing.

Sometimes we smiled when we wanted to cry. We got up early when we wanted to sleep, and packed and went on another trip when we really wanted to stay at home. Both of us left homes that we enjoyed working in, gardens that gave us pleasure, and friends and family whose companionship we valued.

We did it all to do a very simple thing, an *unusually* simple thing. It was not simple to execute—not easy to do—not inexpensive, in all the ways things can be expensive—mentally, physically, financially, emotionally, socially, personally. But it was really a simple, logical thing. We went to see the people we needed to have help us. We went to see

Americans who felt and thought and cared about their lives and their land as we feel and think and care.

A seasoned campaign advance man once remarked to us, "I have worked with other political families, and the women in those families didn't do what you have done. They came to let the people see them. You are here to see the people!" That was it. That's what we did. And in doing that, Rosalynn's and my life became intricately entwined. We shared a dream, and now we are sharing in its fulfillment. It was good then. It is good now.